PENNSYLVANIA COLLEGE OF TECHNOLOGY LIBR

5 0608 01031

D1370959

NEW DIRECTIONS FOR STUDENT SERVICES

Margaret J. Barr, *Northwestern University*
EDITOR-IN-CHIEF

M. Lee Upcraft, *The Pennsylvania State University*
ASSOCIATE EDITOR

Budgeting as a Tool for Policy in Student Affairs

Dudley B. Woodard, Jr.
University of Arizona

EDITOR

Number 70, Summer 1995

JOSSEY-BASS PUBLISHERS
San Francisco

LIBRARY

Pennsylvania College
of Technology

One College Avenue
Williamsport, PA 17701-5799

BUDGETING AS A TOOL FOR POLICY IN STUDENT AFFAIRS
Dudley B. Woodard, Jr. (ed.)
New Directions for Student Services, no. 70
Margaret J. Barr, Editor-in-Chief
M. Lee Upcraft, Associate Editor

© 1995 by Jossey-Bass Inc., Publishers. All rights reserved.

No part of this issue may be reproduced in any form—except for a brief quotation (not to exceed 500 words) in a review or professional work—without permission in writing from the publishers.

Microfilm copies of issues and articles are available in 16mm and 35mm, as well as microfiche in 105mm, through University Microfilms Inc., 300 North Zeeb Road, Ann Arbor, Michigan 48106-1346.

LC 85-644751   ISSN 0164-7970   ISBN 0-7879-9953-9

NEW DIRECTIONS FOR STUDENT SERVICES is part of The Jossey-Bass Higher and Adult Education Series and is published quarterly by Jossey-Bass Inc., Publishers, 350 Sansome Street, San Francisco, California 94104-1342. Second-class postage paid at San Francisco, California, and at additional mailing offices. POSTMASTER: Send address changes to New Directions for Student Services, Jossey-Bass Inc., Publishers, 350 Sansome Street, San Francisco, California 94104-1342.

SUBSCRIPTIONS for 1995 cost $48.00 for individuals and $64.00 for institutions, agencies, and libraries.

EDITORIAL CORRESPONDENCE should be sent to the Editor-in-Chief, Margaret J. Barr, 633 Clark Street, 2-219, Evanston, Illinois 60208-1103.

Cover photograph by Wernher Krutein/PHOTOVAULT © 1990.

Manufactured in the United States of America. Nearly all Jossey-Bass books, jackets, and periodicals are printed on recycled paper that contains at least 50 percent recycled waste, including 10 percent postconsumer waste. Many of our materials are also printed with vegetable-based inks; during the printing process, these inks emit fewer volatile organic compounds (VOCs) than petroleum-based inks. VOCs contribute to the formation of smog.

CONTENTS

EDITOR'S NOTES

The fiscal roller coaster of the 1970s and 1980s prompted many institutions of higher education to tighten their budgets by reducing, consolidating, and merging programs, which reduced human resources and operating costs. The "fiscal woes" lament by the higher education community has not led to any broad-based support but rather has heightened the public debate over the efficiency and effectiveness of higher education.

Article after article (Breneman, 1993; El-Khawas, 1994; Guskin, 1994; Katz and West, 1991) reveals a recurring theme: for higher education to reclaim the public's trust, it must undergo a fundamental restructuring—a shift from an institutional acquisition entrepreneurial model to a student-centered learning model. Simply cutting programs and reallocating resources will not lead to such a fundamental shift. A. E. Guskin (1994, p. 25), chancellor of Antioch University, underscores this point by observing, "Focusing on student learning turns our thinking about the future of our colleges and universities upside-down: from faculty productivity to student productivity, from faculty disciplinary interests to what students need to learn, from faculty teaching styles to student learning styles, from classroom teaching to student learning."

To change the educational culture and create a learning environment that focuses on student learning (outcomes), institutions of higher learning must be willing to rethink organizational structures, curriculum, incentives, and the locus of decision making. Bergquist (1993) refers to this as a postmodern world with less identifiable boundaries. Katz and West (1991, p. 8) describe this new reality as designing American campuses "under a new set of management philosophies and operating principles, . . . a vision that represents a significant departure from existing cultural norms, structure, behaviors, and systems." Conditions must be created that encourage cross-disciplinary discussions without fear of retrenchment and disenfranchisement. As more institutions begin to shift their focus to student learning, the question for student affairs practitioners becomes: How will student services change during restructuring?

This volume of New Directions for Student Services focuses on budgeting as a policy tool for restructuring. Each chapter is written from the perspective of the changing conditions in higher education, that is, moving beyond cost containment through reductions and combinations toward accountability and effectiveness through restructuring.

In Chapter One, Marie Kotter describes a philosophical framework for restructuring the professional roles, processes, and organizational structures in student services. A rationale for making decisions and implementing the practical budget strategies is presented in subsequent chapters. Jo Anne Trow, in Chapter Two, discusses the current and future budgetary climate in higher education. What is the outlook for the foreseeable future? What trends have emerged? How are budgets being used as a tool for restructuring? What is the likely budgetary outlook for student affairs under restructuring? What issues have emerged?

Gary Rhoades, in Chapter Three, offers some penetrating insights on rising administrative costs and various explanations for these increases during the past two decades. Why have administrative costs risen so dramatically during periods of downsizing and budget cutting? What remedies are available for controlling escalating administrative costs? Have costs risen disproportionately among administrative units?

Chapter Four focuses on sources of funding for student affairs services and programs, including appropriated revenue, auxiliary enterprises, fees for services, outsourcing, and sales and services. Stan Levy addresses such questions as: What are the implications for these sources during restructuring? What will be some of the new directions in funding? How does the choice of funding mechanism influence the delivery of student affairs programs and services?

Tom Boyle, in Chapter Five, discusses the sources of information required for sound decision making. His approach is not to itemize lists of sources but rather to encourage the reader to think about the major sources and contexts and how to use the information. What information does the practitioner need to develop budgets under restructuring? Institutional mission? Priorities? Clientele needs? Job market? Financial forecast?

Closely related to information sources for decision making are the criteria necessary to set priorities for funding under restructuring. Jim Gold, in Chapter Six, defines these criteria and offers some advice on their use. What processes should be used to establish criteria? What are some of these criteria? Do any available models exist to assist professionals in this important area? How should they be used?

What are the ethical issues involved in budget development? Choosing between and among competing needs and programs can be very difficult, particularly when decisions involve personnel or changing funding sources (such as moving to fees for services). Patricia Mielke and John Schuh, in Chapter Seven, address these issues and provide an ethical framework for decision making.

Dennis Madson, in Chapter Eight, outlines strategies to develop and sell the student affairs budget during restructuring. Which strategies seem to work and which do not? How do you state consequences of not funding services? To what issues should the practitioner be alert?

The final chapter provides an annotated bibliography that identifies additional sources of information regarding the issues and concepts of our new reality.

The editor acknowledges and appreciates the assistance of Michael Rosenberg in the editing of this volume. Mike recently received his M.A. in higher education from the University of Arizona.

Dudley B. Woodard, Jr.
Editor

References

Breneman, D. W. *Higher Education: On a Collision Course with New Realities.* AGB Occasional Paper, no. 22. Washington, D.C.: Association of Governing Boards of Universities and Colleges, 1993.

Bergquist, W. *The Post Modern Organization.* San Francisco: Jossey-Bass, 1993.

El-Khawas, E. *Restructuring Initiatives in Public Higher Education: Institutional Responses to Financial Constraints.* Research Briefs, vol. 5, no. 8. Washington, D.C.: American Council on Education, 1994.

Guskin, A. E. "Reducing Student Costs and Enhancing Student Learning, Part I: Restructuring the Administration." *Change,* 1994, 26 (4), 23–29.

Katz, R. N., and West, R. P. *Sustaining Excellence in the 21st Century: A Vision and Strategies for College and University Administration.* Boulder, Colo.: CAUSE, 1991.

DUDLEY B. WOODARD, JR., is professor of higher education at the University of Arizona, Tucson. He was vice president of student affairs at SUNY–Binghamton and the University of Arizona and president of NASPA 1989–1990.

This chapter presents a framework for restructuring the professional roles, processes, and organizational structures in student services and provides a rationale for decision making.

Restructuring Student Services: A Philosophical Framework

Marie L. Kotter

Higher education stands at a major crossroads. The choices made today will determine the type, number, and size of higher education institutions in the future. As institutions redesign themselves to meet new demands, student services must also redesign roles, processes, and organizational structures. To ensure that decisions made during this redesign have philosophical integrity and are congruent with the emphasis on measurable student learning, a philosophical framework is required. This chapter provides a framework for student services professionals that can be used as a philosophical rationale for making decisions and implementing the practical budget strategies discussed in the subsequent chapters.

As Langfitt argues (1990, p. 8), "The issues disenchanting the public about health care and higher education—excessive costs, a perceived decline in the quality of the services and inadequate access based mainly on costs—are remarkably similar." If he is correct, and many analysts believe he is, higher education may be ten years away from the transformations now occurring in the health care industry. Hospital physical plants are overbuilt as primary care shifts to clinics and other outpatient facilities. For-profit corporations are buying hospitals across the United States, combining services, closing inefficient and old hospitals, and building new clinics close to their patients. Care has shifted from hospital-centered to patient-centered. Hospitals are now entering partnerships with physicians, insurance companies, and community agencies to keep citizens well. Preventing illness rather than treating sick patients in expensive hospitals is to everyone's best interest. Physicians or hospitals isolated from their community partners will not survive. These changes are driven by economics and the public, despite the defeat of the Clinton Health Care Program.

When the comparison between health care and higher education is examined, the similarities are striking. The argument can be made that health care is a matter of life and death, whereas higher education is voluntary and impacts a smaller number of people and therefore is not as critical to the general public. However, Drucker contends that in the new world, post secondary education is no longer a luxury for the privileged but a basic requirement for survival: "Education will become the center of the knowledge society and the school its key institution. The acquisition and distribution of formal knowledge may come to occupy the place in the politics of the knowledge society which the acquisition and distribution of property and income have occupied in our politics over the two or three centuries that we have come to call the Age of Capitalism" (1994, p. 66).

With higher education elevated to a job survival requirement, the demands for access to low-cost, quality education reach crescendo. Institutions receiving state and federal funds will be required to reduce student costs and enhance student learning, and private institutions will be faced with similar challenges to keep their door open.

Guskin documents these mandates and argues that "colleges and universities face their most significant crisis in over 40 years" (1994b, p. 23). He believes that reducing students' costs and enhancing student learning will force a change in our basic higher education paradigm. Our current model stems from the monasteries of the Middle Ages where knowledge was preserved and passed down to future generations. In this faculty-centered model, the creation and preservation of knowledge was the primary objective—student learning was a secondary objective. With the advent of the printing press, students became even more ancillary to the process, and faculty disciplinary interests and writing became paramount.

Student-Centered Universities and Colleges

Guskin proposes that a new student-centered model of higher education with the emphasis on student learning is now required. "Focusing on student learning turns our thinking about the future of our colleges and universities upside down: from faculty productivity to student productivity, from faculty disciplinary interests to what students need to learn, from faculty teaching styles to student learning styles, from classroom teaching to student learning" (1994b, p. 25).

What will higher education institutions look like in the future? The top-tier state research institutions may narrow their mission to graduate student education and research and withdraw completely from undergraduate education. Fred J. Evans, dean of the College of Business Administration at Eastern Washington University, states that state funding has decreased dramatically and regulations have increased. He recommends eliminating remaining state support to subsidize tuition costs and increasing tuition to the same level for all students. Community colleges are already much more responsive to community needs, and many are totally supported by district voters. Their mission and share of the educational market will continue to increase as more and more first-generation students begin their higher education experience at low-cost, open admission, student-centered institutions.

The real question is what will four-year colleges and university undergraduate institutions do in this new world? Institutions that understand the new reality of the student-centered paradigm and already have a strong reputation with students and their parents may thrive. Others may suffer through unending rounds of budget reductions and student enrollment decreases until they close their doors.

The pressure of increasing costs of education, coupled with demands for access and enhanced learning outcomes and rapid advances in technology, will force radical change in the administrative and educational practices of American higher education. Guskin warns that "implementation of radical alterations in all administrative areas must proceed implementation of major changes in the role of faculty" (1994a, p. 29). He maintains that administrative reductions will not produce enough savings to reduce student costs, and significant increases in faculty productivity are only possible by fundamentally restructuring the work of faculty members. While this restructuring is occurring, the pressure on administration, particularly student services, will continue to increase. As faculty push for the same level of restructuring in all areas of the campus, the spotlight will intensify on student services divisions. Many student services are already perceived by some faculty as nonessential to the academic mission. As student learning becomes the central institutional focus, the division that traditionally has advocated and articulated the student point of view runs the risk of isolation. However, student services professionals can become important leaders and facilitators of this change if they lead the way with restructuring and assessing the outcomes of their own work.

"Restructuring the role of faculty members will at first prove to be a monumental undertaking. All of the incentives seem against doing so—except, in the end, survival" (Guskin, 1994b, p. 25). When faculty are dealing with survival issues, the political climate for other members of the campus community will be perilous. Student service professionals must be aware of these issues and take steps now to help create learning environments, enhance student learning through peer interaction, and assess the outcomes of their efforts.

Model for Restructuring Student Services Professional Role

Guskin's model for restructuring the faculty role in the new learner-centered colleges and universities can be used to restructure the role of the student services professional as well. (See Table 1.1.)

Table 1.1. Restructured SS Role and Use of New Technologies.

Types of Student Learning	Faculty Role	Student Services Professional Role	Peer-Group Role/Individual Learning	Technology
Accumulation of knowledge and information	Presenter; assessor of learning; faculty or librarian as guide to resources	Educator and resource to campus for: information about students and their learning styles; environmental designs and programs to enhance learning of values; attitudes and behaviors such as multiculturalism, relativistic commitments, spiritual and physical development	Independent learning; use of guides to access new technology and help with independent learning	Interactive technologies; access to databases; communication technology network with others throughout the country
Skill development	Coach outside class; group discussion leader; trainer of student coaches	Advisor and trainer for individuals and groups; educator for developmental skills such as conflict resolution, planning and organizing, delegation and control	Older and more experienced peers as coaches; action settings using skills	Interactive technologies; computer simulation
Conceptual development	Mentor and model; small group discussion leader; convener of cooperative learning groups; one-on-one advising; faculty-student interaction	Mentor and model; coach/advisor and designer of opportunities to enhance conceptual learning; one-on-one advising	Peer-group interaction; cooperative learning groups; testing ideas in real-life experience; independent learning	Simulation/virtual reality; human simulation; communication technology networks
Personal/social development	Role model in student's academic major; advising for academic career goals	Role model, as a professional and as a person; advising for personal, social, and career goals; assessing developmental task competencies and achievements	Older more experienced peers as student leaders; student peer-group interactions in clubs, organizations, residence halls, volunteer programs	Communication networks used to contact other students in class, on campus, across the United States, and the world. Network used to solicit student

Source: Adapted from Guskin, 1994c.

Guskin uses learning strategies from Norman (1993) to define the faculty role in different types of learning. In the category "accumulation of knowledge and information," Guskin sees the faculty as the guide to learning resources and the assessor of learning. In this design, a "course" may consist of "learning blocks" composed of electronic resources, intensive interaction with a faculty member, intensive lecture discussion periods, simulations or internships, and peer study groups. Evaluations of the learning in each block will be integrated into a total assessment of learning (Guskin, 1994b, p. 21).

Student services professionals will be designers of opportunities and campus environments to enhance learning. They will serve as campus resources to provide information about a particular campus's students and their learning styles. Cocurricular learning opportunities will be particularly important in student learning of values, attitudes, and behaviors, such as multiculturalism, relativistic commitments, and spiritual and physical development.

High-level skill development is a focus of much of the faculty's work. In addition to the "learning block courses," Guskin describes faculty acting as coaches outside the classroom, trainers of student coaches, and as group discussion leaders (1994b, p. 21). Student services professionals also will be acting as advisors, trainers, and coaches for individual students and student groups in such skills as conflict resolution, planning and organizing, delegation, and control. These skills have been identified by California State University (CSU), the American Assembly of Collegiate Schools of Business (AACSB), and the Southern Association of Colleges and Schools (SACS) as desirable learning outcomes.

Conceptual development requires faculty to use instructional strategies that motivate students to engage in reflective leaning to form conceptual structures. Guskin believes this will require faculty "to integrate the new world of simulation and interactive technologies with their own unique role as mentors, coaches, facilitators and guides of student learning" (1994b, p. 23). One-on-one advising and faculty-student interaction are powerful ways to encourage students to see how learning interacts with other learning and with future career goals. He challenges faculty members to use simulations and personal contact to help students achieve this level of motivation so they will do the hard work and reflection necessary to do conceptual development (Guskin, 1994b, p. 23). Students also will be learning concepts independently and with peers. Conceptual development processes vary with individual learning styles. Some students can reflect more effectively alone, whereas others need to work within small peer groups. Faculty legitimization of this type of learning is important for conceptual development to take place.

Conceptual development is critical in the developmental themes that are the bedrock of the student services professionals' role as an educator. Winston and Miller (1994) have identified developmental outcome taxonomies that can be used to identify these developmental themes. Winston and Miller (1994, p. 4) draw on the academic and intellectual themes identified by Bloom (1956),

Bowen (1977), and Boyer (1987), and in addition use Chickering (1969), Pascarella and Terenzini (1991), California State University (1989), American Assembly of Collegiate Schools of Business (1987), and Southern Association of Colleges and Schools (1992) to identify those themes important to student affairs programs and services. (See Table 1.2.) These include cultural literacy and tolerance, spiritual or moral development, salubrious lifestyle, and commitment to realism in the intellectual domain. In these areas, the student services professional will act as a model and coach/advisor for students and as designer of programs, services, and learning environments to motivate students to complete their conceptual development in these areas.

An additional category, identified by Winston and Miller but not by Guskin, is personal/social development. In this category, the faculty role in one-on-one advising described by Guskin in the conceptual development area will be very important. Faculty act as role models in the students' academic major and should meet regularly with students to advise and help students establish academic career goals. Student services professionals also are powerful role models. They work with students to identify personal, social, and career goals and facilitate sexual identity, interdependence, personality characteristics, and life coping skills in the emotional category. In addition, intimacy, empathy, citizenship, and civility are important outcomes in the social interpersonal component and can result from programs and services designed by student services professionals.

Holistic Student Assessment. Guskin argues that the "restructuring of the faculty role over the next 5 to 10 years will require significant changes in assessment procedures. If the primary focus of colleges and universities will be on student learning which occurs in a number of different settings—intense faculty/student interaction, teams of peers, use of interactive technologies and reflection on experience—student assessment must focus on individual students and what they have learned" (1994b, p. 25).

The need for holistic assessment of individual student learning and development will impact student affairs programs and services. Winston and Miller propose a holistic model for assessment of both academic and student affairs components. Holistic assessment plans will be necessary to document to the public, the students, and the campus community that learning has taken place. Winston and Miller also address the politics of outcomes assessment. The politics of how, who, and what are assessed is a subset of the politics inherent in restructuring universities and colleges (Winston and Miller, 1994).

Borden and Bottrill (1994, p. 18) indicate that performance indicators can be used to focus and strengthen an organization's improvement efforts by helping to communicate a common institutional mission and goals among constituent units, convey institutional priorities, and set standards for performance and accountability. They also comment that the use of performance indicators is a highly political issue.

Banta and Borden (1994, p. 104) maintain that experiences in Europe and

Table 1.2. Developmental Outcome Taxonomies

Developmental Themes	Bloom (1956)	Bowen (1977)	Boyer (1987)	Chickering (1969)	Pascarella and Terenzini (1991)	CSU (1989)	AACSB (1987)	SACS (1987)
Academic	Knowledge Comprehension	Verbal and quantitative skills Substantive knowledge	Grasp of field of endeavor Well-rounded general education	Academic competence	Academic self-concept Educational attainments	Communication skills	Communication skills	Retention and completion Academic achievement Graduate education
Cultural		Cultural sensitivity			Aesthetic and cultural values	Sensitivity for multicultural diversity Aesthetic appreciation		
Emotional				Managing emotions Autonomy Identity		Self-awareness Positive self-concept	Self-objectivity	Affective development
Intellectual	Application Analysis Synthesis Evaluation	Rationality Intellectual tolerance Wisdom Intellectual integrity			Intellectual values Political and social liberalism	Critical thinking and analysis	Planning and organization skills Problem analysis	
Moral				Integrity	Secularism	Ethical judgment Social commitment		
Physical				Physical competence				
Purpose			Career training and skills for-mulating life goals	Clarified purpose	Career choice mobility and success Educational aspirations	Career coping skills		Accomplishing educational objectives Job placement rates
Social-interpersonal			Getting along with others	Social competence Free interpersonal relationships		Negotiation skills Interpersonal skills Coping skills	Leadership skills Delegation and control Disposition to lead	Social recognition of achievement

Note: CSU=California State University, AACSB=American Assembly of Collegiate Schools of Business, SACS=Southern Association of Colleges and Schools (Winston and Miller 1994, p.4).

the United States show, "Efforts to choose performance indicators without regard to how they can or will be used are doomed to failure. This lesson holds true as well for efforts to use performance indicators that have not been chosen carefully by those who must ultimately use the resulting information to improve program, institutional or system performance." They list five criteria for judging performance indicators: purpose and alignment across inputs, processes and outcomes, coordination throughout the system, coordination of methods, and use in decision making. These five criteria address both choice and usage issues.

Redesigned Learning-Oriented Student Affairs Divisions. Guskin suggests reducing administrative and student services expenses by 25 to 33 percent and the size of the faculty by 25 to 33 percent. He believes that this magnitude of restructuring is necessary to hold down student costs and argues that carrying out these changes creatively could accomplish cost reduction while enhancing student learning (1994b, p. 25).

The 33 percent decrease in budgetary support is in addition to any state-supported institutional cuts that have been mandated by decreased taxpayer support in many states. If we continue to do business as usual, we will end up slashing and burning academic, administrative, and student services programs with negative effects on student learning, which will cause economic citizen mandates directly targeted at higher education.

The American College Personnel Association (1994) reiterates the transformation of higher education and challenges student affairs professionals to design and implement a learning-oriented student affairs division. They identify the following characteristics of such a division:

> (1) The student affairs division mission complements the institution's mission with the enhancement of student learning and personal development being the primary goal of student affairs programs and services; (2) Resources are allocated to encourage student learning and personal development; (3) Student affairs professionals collaborate with other institutional agents and agencies to promote student learning and personal development; (4) The division of student affairs includes staff who are experts on students, their environments, and teaching and learning processes; (5) Student affairs policies and programs are based on promising practices from the research on student learning and institution specific assessment data. [pp. 2–4]

Like Guskin, leaders in student affairs recommend redesigning our work, which will reconfigure our budgets. As Plato said, "The new approach becomes the dominant approach as the need for change is satisfied" (Plato, 1978, p. 34). The budgeting process can be used as one of the driving forces in restructuring efforts. The chapters that follow illustrate concrete ways to use budgeting to accomplish the major changes required to move student affairs into a more learning-oriented structure.

References

American Assembly of Collegiate Schools of Business. "Outcomes Measurement Project, Phase 3 Report." St. Louis, Mo.: American Assembly of Collegiate Schools of Business, 1987.

American College Personnel Association. *The Student Learning Imperative: Implications for Student Affairs*. Washington, D.C.: American College Personnel Association, 1994.

Banta, T. W., and Borden, V.M.H. "Performance Indicators for Accountability and Improvement." *Using Performance Indicators to Guide Strategic Decision Making*. New Directions for Institutional Research, no. 82. San Francisco: Jossey-Bass, 1994.

Bloom, B. S. and Associates. *Taxonomy of Educational Objectives*. New York: McKay, 1956.

Borden, V.M.H., and Bottrill, K. V. "Performance Indicators: History, Definitions, and Methods." *Using Performance Indicators to Guide Strategic Decision Making*. New Directions for Institutional Research, no. 82. San Francisco: Jossey-Bass, 1994.

Bowen, H. R. *Investment in Learning: The Individual and Social Value of American Higher Education*. San Francisco: Jossey-Bass, 1977.

Boyer, E. *The Undergraduate Experience in America*. New York: Harper & Row, 1987.

California State University. "Report of the Educational Support Services Master Plan Task Force." Long Beach, Calif.: Academic Affairs, Educational Support, Office of the Chancellor, 1989.

Chickering, A. W. *Education and Identity*. San Francisco: Jossey-Bass, 1969.

Drucker, P. F. "The Age of Social Transformation." *Atlantic Monthly*, 1994, *274* (5), 53–80.

Evans, F. J. "The Coming Privatization of Public Higher Education." Unpublished paper, Eastern Washington University.

Guskin, A. E. "Reducing Student Costs and Enhancing Student Learning, Part I: Restructuring the Administration." *Change*, 1994a, *26* (4), 23–29.

Guskin, A. E. "Reducing Student Costs and Enhancing Student Learning, Part II: Restructuring the Role of Faculty." *Change*, 1994b, *26* (5), 16–25.

Guskin, A .E. "Restructuring Faculty Work: More Learning for Fewer Bucks." *Change*, 1994c, *26* (5).

Langfitt, T. W. "The Cost of Higher Education: Lessons to Learn from the Health Care Industry." *Change*, 1990, *22* (6), 8–15.

Norman, D. *Things That Make Us Smart: Defending Human Attributes in the Age of the Machine*. Reading, Mass.: Addison Wesley, 1993.

Pascarella, E. T., and Terenzini, P. T. *How College Affects Students: Findings and Insights from Twenty Years of Research*. San Francisco: Jossey-Bass, 1991.

Plato, K. "The Shift to Student Development: An Analysis of the Patterns of Change." *NASPA Journal*, 1978, *15* (4), 32–36.

Southern Association of Colleges and Schools. *Criteria for Accreditation*. Decatur, Ga.: Commission of Colleges, Southern Association of Colleges and Schools, 1992.

Winston, R. B., Jr., and Miller, T. K. "A Model for Assessing Developmental Outcomes Related to Student Affairs Programs and Services." *NASPA Journal*, 1994, *32* (1), 2–18.

MARIE L. KOTTER *is vice president for student services at Weber State University, Ogden, Utah.*

The current and future budgetary climate in higher education is discussed in relation to trends, emerging issues, budget influence on restructuring, and relationships to larger institutional issues.

Budgetary Climate

Jo Anne Trow

In a large western state, an initiative lowered taxes and deliberately limited state spending, necessitating multimillion-dollar budget reductions in four-year state colleges and universities. Travel funds were frozen, some new positions were not approved, and others were eliminated. In another state, the higher education coordinating board and the legislature proposed a system of funding based on performance toward statewide goals ranked in importance by legislative leaders (Ashworth, 1994). In yet another state, a combination of economic issues, voter-initiated efforts to reduce property taxes, and concerns for public safety and corrections programs resulted in reductions for higher education in succeeding biennia of 2 percent, 12 percent, 20 percent, and 13 percent. In other states, productivity goals were established and incentive funding initiated or report cards on effectiveness ordered. The private sector, hit hard by a decade of steep tuition increases resulting in a widening of the gap between public and private tuition, has had to find additional revenue sources and reduce costs by reorganizing administrative units and cutting academic programs.

These examples graphically reflect the climate of higher education and the increasing calls for accountability, outcomes assessment, and governmental regulations and reporting requirements that place additional demands on already slim budgets. This chapter will provide an overview of these concerns by examining the current financial condition of higher education, suggesting ways the budgeting process can lead to creative and responsive restructuring, and looking at trends in student services budgeting.

Outlook and Trends

Higher education faces increasing criticism for what it is and is not doing. Deep public concern exists. Students and parents find themselves "overwhelmed with sticker shock" (Wingspread Group on Higher Education, 1993). The concern for "learning productivity," as cost begins to exceed reach, may change the structure and culture of higher education. Technology presents continuing challenges and exciting possibilities. Increased expectations for accountability, outcomes assessment, and performance-based funding have altered the familiar incremental budgeting systems. Competition for limited resources is fierce, especially in the face of increasing demands for services and programs. At the same time, this competition challenges institutions to increase the effectiveness of student affairs programs—especially retention programs. To paraphrase Dickens, for higher education this can be the worst of times and the best of times.

The American Council on Education reported that by spring 1994 more than two-thirds of the public institutions of higher education had undertaken serious steps to reduce expenditures and redirect programs. Widespread action tightened expenditure controls by increased monitoring of expenses and concerted efforts to develop new sources of revenue. More than half of all institutions of higher education had reorganization and restructuring underway, affecting both academic and administrative units. Among larger institutions, one-half of doctoral granting and research universities and at least one-third of community colleges and comprehensive institutions had taken actions to control expenditures, reorganize, seek new sources of revenue, and make changes in academic programs.

Coupled with these reductions and reallocations is the concern for the rising cost of education, with the subsequent increased tuition charges for the students (El-Khawas, 1994). Breneman (1994) suggests that state support of public higher education will continue to decline and that options must be found for use of limited state dollars. Shifting state support from institutions into need-based student aid could result in public universities raising tuition to make up for reduced state support. Another scenario would be to increase budget efficiency of state-assisted institutions by focusing on outcomes and contractual agreements with the state rather than on the accounting and regulatory control of inputs. The movement toward increasing decentralization of responsibility and eliminating unnecessary, anachronistic, or overly complex policies focuses revenues on programs rather than actual delivery process.

Current Climate. The current budgetary climate of student affairs can be characterized as tentative, cautiously optimistic, competitive, depressing, or uncertain. Many institutions, particularly those dependent on public funding, are experiencing declining revenues along with increased expectations. The average level of state appropriations in the last several years has remained fairly constant, but inflation has negated real increases in operating budgets. Overall, appropriations have been reduced even with a demand for additional services (National Association of State Universities and Land Grant Colleges, 1994). Tuition increases required to meet instructional and service needs of higher education drive up the costs for the consumer. As a consequence, student debt burden increases and enrollment is negatively affected. This contradiction between the commitment to access and the realities of limited capacity to serve more students without jeopardizing traditional concepts of quality plagues many campuses (National Center for Higher Education Management Systems, 1994). Some institutions are limiting enrollments by increasing entrance requirements and restricting access to particular programs such as engineering and business and popular undergraduate liberal arts majors such as psychology. Thirty-four percent of public four-year higher education institutions have taken steps to limit enrollments in some way (National Association of State Universities, 1994). The demand to provide measurable outcomes is increasingly becoming the means to allocate resources. Competition for these limited resources is considerable and demands more careful application of general accountability and outcomes assessment processes.

Garland and Grace (1993) believe that cost cutting concerns can be minimized if organizations demonstrate that they are cost effective, that they have explored other sources of revenue, and that their efforts lead to students' achievement and persistence. Some have advised asking or requiring faculty to assume their former roles of advising and counseling students.

Trends in Budgeting Processes. Reliance on practices previously used only in the business world is increasingly a tool for resource allocation. Total Quality Management, "continuous improvement," benchmarking, and process reengineering or business process redesigning will continue as the focus of the means for general restructuring (Lombardo and Pappas, 1992). These processes are labor-intensive to implement, but the ultimate purpose is generally stated as providing a business tool to increase productivity and thereby better customer service.

Technology and its increasing demands for equipment, changes in infrastructure, staff training, and attitude modification create significant new budgetary pressures. The change in service delivery and the needs of the ever-changing student body present additional demands. Katz and West, in describing their "network" vision for higher education, emphasize the importance in investing information technology infrastructure as a key determinant in administrative excellence (Katz and West, 1994).

The changes in expectations of operating procedures within the organization cause additional ambiguities and apprehensions. Traditional and hierarchical organizations are being flattened, with fewer managers and more reliance on networking. Initiative is still welcome, but the demand for teamwork is more pronounced. The decentralization of the organizational structure creates new opportunities, but at the same time raises concerns. Changing the culture can be a time-consuming exercise—it demands rethinking processes that influence the way resources are used. More emphasis is currently directed toward cost containment (growth by substitution) rather than the cost plus (increases for the base and for new programs) environment. Fiscal leaders remain optimistic about finances, but institution-wide budget cuts, increased use of part-time employees, and sophisticated management information services create a different environment for student affairs. Costs have risen faster than inflation, loans outstrip stipends and grants, and the increased demands on state resources by other agencies such as health and public safety have resulted in reduced allocations to higher education (Woodard, 1993).

Budgeting as a Tool for Restructuring

Reductions in budgets often have been merely an across-the-board general reduction in every department's budget level. This approach can mean reducing services, cutting back on hours, laying off staff, closing down summer programs, relying more on part-time help, or any of the other traditional ways of implementing budget reductions. On the other hand, budget reductions can be a positive force in an organization as a tool for restructuring. More specific strategies are discussed later in this volume, but it is useful in a general discussion on budgetary climate to look at some areas where rethinking service delivery can be more productive than reducing the levels of service.

Within the workplace, personnel and other organizational demands impact budget decisions. Changes in organizational structures from traditional hierarchical organizations to flatter organizations dependent on networks rather than the usual line and staff relationships affect the way money is allocated and managed. Worker expectations influencing the way work is performed traditionally focus on job security. Now, opportunities for professional development for job satisfaction are a concern. The application of quality management programs and the resulting reengineering or redesigning of processes are significant and useful on many campuses.

Budgetary reductions can force student affairs organizations to rethink the way they operate, staff their programs, and perceive their institutional role. If the budget reduction process allows the time, the opportunity to rework position descriptions and staff assignments may help identify the most effective methods to meet the needs of the changing student body. Savings often result from consolidating positions and responsibilities. At the same time, some situations may require elimination of services or positions. The American Council on Education's recent study on responses to funding cuts indicated several areas of significance to student services. The most likely actions institutions take to meet financial crisis are expenditure control, developing new sources of revenue, and restructuring and setting priorities among academic programs. However, doctoral granting universities and research universities are more likely to levy new fees and reorganize student services as a cost-cutting measure. Community colleges and comprehensive universities are less likely to take this approach. Nevertheless, over half the respondents in this study target student services reorganization (El-Khawas, 1994).

Budget reductions may be used as a rationale to examine potentially taboo changes, such as departmental boundaries and traditional services deliveries that have evolved over the years around incumbents. Departments develop their own specialized courses in a general subject such as statistics or mathematics rather than using the course taught in the regular department. Student affairs departments develop their own specialists within each department, such as handling group advising and business operations. Counseling services often exist in a number of different departments. Student organization advising and leadership development training programs may be carried out by a number of different offices. Career planning is often performed in both placement and counseling centers. These specialties may be more appropriately located in other departments within the student affairs unit. Consolidating and coordinating services can conserve resources and offer more effective program delivery. At the same time, dean of students' offices have frequently become the catch-all—gradually picking up a variety of unrelated or unclaimed services and programs. Evaluating the services and the departmental boundaries existing around these activities might be a way to address the budgetary needs and the needs of students.

Creative thinking about unorthodox mergers of programs, activities, and departments that move across traditional boundaries may save money, provide more relevant services, and energize staff with new responsibilities and possibilities for staff development and personal growth. Each campus culture dictates natural mergers, but ones not readily apparent generally pay off in productivity, decreased costs, and increased student satisfaction. The latter is true especially if students are involved in planning and implementing the program. For example, staff in an activity center envisioned using a retirement to completely reorganize center staffing and operation. Discussions with staff and students showed that a number of practices had served them well and should be continued. Although not all student recommendations were carried out, student involvement had significant impact on the final staffing plan. Students felt significant ownership in the outcome and a renewed interest in center programs.

Also important are alliances with areas directly related to student affairs but not used in the past. A common example of an alliance with an academic area is the use of counseling students as interns in the counseling center. Working out shared staff responsibilities or shared student programming with nearby institutions could result in cost savings or the possibility of additional income and enhancement of programs. For example, sharing student media facilities with nearby institutions that do not have as sophisticated physical facilities could provide income as well as additional opportunities for staff. Discussions with academic colleagues can provide input on how student affairs staff with expertise can augment instructional programs and build relationships that benefit student affairs.

Forging new alliances with others in the academic community and the community at large is important for a number of reasons. They may provide additional sources of income and create opportunities to work with colleagues in focusing on the importance of student services in the total student learning arena. Such alliances can help student services operations and bring additional support to instructional areas. The student affairs professional must focus on the benefits of student learning within the university. Since the peer group is the single most powerful influence on student academic and personal development

(Astin, 1993), student affairs professionals must maintain their ability to provide vehicles for this development.

Issues. The issues we face as we work within the restrictions forced on us by budget reductions and reallocations are at times overwhelming as well as challenging. The opportunities to look ahead to new and useful ways of doing things are many. Change can be seen as a harbinger of renewal, not necessarily a premonition of death (Penney, 1993). Student affairs units must learn to quantify the work done in terms of clearly stated outcomes in order to justify continued or increased expenditures. Clearly articulating program outcomes and the consequences of reduced spending can significantly affect the climate where we work and the attitudes of those around us (Barr, 1988).

If student affairs is not viewed as central, the support for student affairs may be deleted by lumping it together with other administrative units. One state system of higher education persists in including student support services as part of administration—along with business operations and custodial services. The resulting mandate to take a major portion of budget reductions from administration forced a significantly higher proportion of reductions for student services than for instructional and teaching staff. Obviously, this negatively impacts student affairs units. Education of the institution at large and particularly of major decision makers is important to overcome this attitude. Barr (1988) indicates that insufficient training in fiscal management has been an issue with student services managers; many are not able to grasp the implications of budget reductions before they are implemented.

Translating or selling the teaching methods used in student affairs to the academic side of the institution is another challenge. Relating the activities in student affairs to the overall mission of the institution, rather than just that of student services divisions, is imperative in order to maintain visibility and credibility within the institution.

Even though most research on student success and satisfaction has been done on traditional age students on traditional residential campuses, one cannot overemphasize the importance of focusing program development and service delivery with the subsequent follow-up and evaluation on the growing proportion of nontraditional students. Developing programs for these students can assist in maintaining existing and securing new resources to serve the new majority participants in American higher education.

The largest cost reductions come from elimination of functions. Student affairs operations seem expendable if they are seen by faculty and administrators as logical for elimination or as irrelevant to the educational process. Constantly documenting and demonstrating how student affairs contributes to the overall success of the student, and thereby the institution, are necessary to prove relevance.

In addition, the pressure to establish fee-for-service or separate-fee-funded programs is more significant in the student services area than in many others (Schuh, 1990). In fact, self-supporting activities may be expected to fund programs other than their own as budgets are reduced and reallocated in those areas. Resisting unnecessary fee assessment for services previously received through tuition and other general support dollars is an important budgetary consideration.

Changing the entire structure, culture, and landscape of higher education and the area of student services are the increased pressures to complete one's education in less than the traditional four years; to approach teaching and learning by individually paced and mastery learning, discouraging excessive experimentation and drift, and encouraging year-round study; and to begin graduate and professional education earlier (Johnstone, 1993). A very different array of services will be needed to meet the needs of this very different culture.

The percentage of overall expenditures in an institutional budget for student affairs ranges from 3 to 10 percent, depending on the size of the institution. Regardless of the percentage of the allocation, the importance of student services cannot be relegated to a lesser level based merely on that distribution. The challenge for student affairs is to sustain its advantage in the face of acute financial problems that could undermine the last two centuries of work. Student services organizations need to rethink what they do and how they do it, keeping in mind that higher education perhaps cannot afford to be what it has become (Shafer and Coate, 1992). We must change the strategic focus of our organizations to capitalize on the opportunities, taking the lead in restructuring traditional organizations to meet the needs of nontraditional students, and partnering with other institutions and agencies as programs are developed and retooled to make the most of the resources we have available.

Outlook for the Future

The budgetary outlook for higher education in general is problematic. Unpredictable timing of reductions hinders planning, creates lost opportunities, and wreaks havoc on carefully developed formula allocation models. Constant budget reductions and reallocation orders create time-consuming exercises and serious morale problems in trying to project various levels of cuts when the actual numbers do not exist. The size or timing of cuts can create a sense of loss of control. Managing decline is a stress-producing activity (Penney, 1993). The usual range of problems that student affairs has faced pales before the budget realities of reductions, reallocations, and retrenchment (Nuss, 1994). New collaborative approaches to problem solving and program delivery are imperative.

Public scrutiny, calls for accountability, and general targeting of student services as natural for elimination have been part of the retrenchment strategies for well over a decade (Williamson and Mamarchev, 1990). Accountability issues are demonstrated in increasing efforts on the part of states to impose performance-based funding and assessment models on higher education. Texas, Colorado, Tennessee, Arkansas, Missouri, West Virginia, and South Carolina are some of the states implementing effectiveness reports, performance-based or incentive funding, productivity goals, and similar funding procedures in higher education (Ashworth, 1994). The federal government implementation of the State Post-Secondary Review Entities to undertake reviews of institutions having high loan default rates or other triggering criteria is an attempt to assess the outcomes of higher education and establish criteria for funding allocation. Higher education no longer makes its own rules but responds to outside pressures and requirements.

A proactive rather than a reactive stance is imperative. Student affairs can be at the forefront within their institutions in restructuring programs to meet current needs. Madson discusses this further in Chapter Eight.

Program does not appear to be able to influence budget as much as budget now influences program. New staffing needs cannot be automatically covered as frequently budget will dictate the level of staff and thereby the level of service that can be provided. Student affairs operations will find themselves transferring many programs to a self-support status. Traditionally, student housing, some student health, and some student activities operations have been supported with user fees or special student fees. More institutions will find themselves looking not only to additional self-support operations such as counseling, career services, and orientation but to outsourcing or contracting. Contracting out services such as food operations, custodial services, health services, and utilities and instituting student debit cards can generate additional revenue without imposing new costs. Using the expertise of existing staff to run summer programs and conferences in sports, media, leadership development, and other areas related to their training and background can generate additional money. Using private business to remodel and maintain existing buildings and construct new buildings also can save scarce resources (Garland and Grace, 1993). The implications of these strategies are detailed by Levy and Boyle in Chapters Four and Five.

Information technology, although initially expensive, can ultimately lead to more cost effective methods of programming, more sophisticated student information systems, increased productivity, better planning, and better ways of doing business. This is but one example of rising administrative costs that are explored in more detail by Rhoades in Chapter Three.

Alternative sources of revenue can supplement diminishing institutional resources. Many student affairs offices now have sophisticated development operations that seek outside funds for specific programs, buildings, and equipment as well as general operations.

Student affairs operations may have to look closely at reducing the scope of their operations in an attempt to contain costs. Any organization should consider retrenchment and reductions in relation to its mission and strategic plan, the demand for services, level of self-support possible, whether services are available elsewhere, whether elimination would merely transfer responsibility to another unit without significant overall cost savings, and whether academic programs would be affected (Oregon State University, 1992).

Summary

Student services continues to face serious financial constraints. The need to seek new sources of revenue, exercise tight expenditure controls, look seriously at and evaluate the services and programs provided, and establish priorities within the institution is shaped by declining resources and increased expectations for accountability and successful outcomes on the part of the public. In addition, new demands exist from increased technology requirements, additional government regulations and requirements, and the ever-changing demographics of the student population. Diminished public support that does not keep pace with costs, increased loan burdens for students, and increased public demand for outcomes-based education are other concerns.

Student services must use reallocation, retrenchment, and reduction as tools to positively restructure the programs and staff expectations. Confronting the issues of contracting, outsourcing, developing outcomes and assessment measures, and maintaining the role of making a viable contribution to the institution's overall mission requires considerable effort and creative thought on the part of student services administrators. Playing a significant part in the development of strategic plans and tying budget decisions to those plans can help assure that student services survive.

Merely justifying their existence through the impact of student services on retention and graduation rates and the impact on overall student satisfaction will not assure success; student services must demonstrate judicious use of allocated resources and an ability to restructure programs and services to address the social, economic, and demographic challenges in higher education today.

References

Ashworth, K. H. "The Texas Case Study." *Change*, 1994, *26* (6), 8–15.

Astin, A. W. *What Matters in College: Four Critical Years Revisited.* San Francisco: Jossey-Bass, 1993.

Barr, M. J. "Managing Money." In M. J. Barr and M. L. Upcraft (eds.), *Managing Student Affairs Effectively.* New Directions for Student Services, no. 41. San Francisco: Jossey-Bass, 1988.

Breneman, D. W. *Higher Education: On a Collision Course with New Realities.* AGB Occasional Paper, no. 22. Washington, D.C.: Association of Governing Boards of Universities and Colleges, 1994.

El-Khawas, E. *Restructuring Initiatives in Public Higher Education: Institutional Responses to Financial Constraints.* Research Briefs, vol. 5, no. 8. Washington, D.C.: American Council on Education, 1994.

Garland, P. H., and Grace, T. W. *New Perspectives for Student Affairs Professionals.* ASHE–ERIC Higher Education Report, no. 7. Washington, D.C.: George Washington University, 1993.

Institutional Procedures and Criteria for Program Reduction, Reorganization, Reduction and Termination. Corvallis: Oregon State University, 1992.

Johnstone, D. B. "Enhancing the Productivity of Learning." *AAHE Bulletin,* 1993, *46* (4) 3–5.

Katz, R. N., and West, R. P. *Sustaining Excellence in the 21st Century: A Vision and Strategies for College and University Administration.* Boulder, Colo.: CAUSE, 1991.

Lombardo, B. J., and Pappas, A. T. "Facing the Challenge: Reengineering at Oregon State University." *KPMG Peat Marwick Management Issues*, December, 1992.

National Association of State Universities and Land Grant Colleges. *In Brief.* National Association of State Universities and Land Grant Colleges, July, 1994.

National Center for Higher Education Management Systems. "Designing State Policy for New Higher Education Environment." *NCHEM Newsletter*, 1994, *10*.

Nuss, E. M. "Leadership in Higher Education: Confronting the Realities of the 1990s." *NASPA Journal*, 1994, *31* (3), 209–216.

Penney, S. H. "What a University Has Learned from 4 Years of Financial Stress." *Chronicle of Higher Education*, May 5, 1993, B1–3.

Schuh, J. H. "Current Fiscal and Budgetary Perspectives." In J. H. Schuh (ed.), *Financial Management for Student Affairs*. Washington, D.C.: American College Personnel Association, Media, 1990.

Shafer, B. S., and Coate, L. E. "Benchmarking in Higher Education." *NACUBO Business Officer*, 1992, *10* (5), 28–35.

Williamson, M. L., and Mamarchev, H. L. "A Systems Approach to Financial Management for Student Affairs." *NASPA Journal*, 1990, *27* (3), 199–205.

Wingspread Group on Higher Education. *An American Imperative*. Johnson Foundation, 1993.

Woodard, D. B. "Budgeting and Fiscal Management." In M. Barr and Associates, *The Handbook of Student Affairs Administration*. San Francisco: Jossey-Bass, 1993.

Jo Anne Trow is vice president for student affairs at Oregon State University.

This chapter discusses the rising costs of administration and considers the place of student services within restructured institutions.

Rising, Stratified Administrative Costs: Student Services' Place

Gary Rhoades

Conventional wisdom holds that a major factor in the rising costs of higher education is expanded student services—for example, in advising and in services for new populations of students. Such accounts are consistent with public criticism of faculty for reducing the time they devote to students. They are also consistent with prevailing stories of student services' history growth (Hirt, 1992). Limited research exists, however, on disproportionate increases in administrative expenditures. This chapter explores three dimensions of students services' "place" in rising administrative costs: (1) place in the administrative hierarchy—student services' share of administrative expenditure increases relative to other branches of administration; (2) place in the institution—the extent to which student services are being cut or privatized; and (3) place in relation to students—the extent to which student services are reconceptualizing the relationship between provider and client.

The first dimension is vertical. What is the place of student services in the administrative hierarchy in terms of salaries and positions? Within student services the tendency is to focus on the status of the occupation relative to the academic profession instead of stratification among branches of administration. In recent decades, administration has become increasingly professionalized as it has become a full-time career in a full-blown campus bureaucracy. Student services was the first branch of higher education administration to professionalize in the classical sense, for example, developing a knowledge base, specialized training, and a code of ethics. Arguably, it is still the most professionalized. Yet other administrative occupations have professionalized as other pre-existing professions (for example, accounting and law) have been incorporated into higher education administration. Professions are stratified, internally and in relation to other professions (Heinz and Laumann, 1982; Larson, 1977), and evidence exists of increased hierarchy within and among professions. The academic profession is a prime example, with salaries of faculty in different fields of study becoming increasingly dispersed (Slaughter and Rhoades, 1994). One might expect professional status to be related to age and technical knowledge base. However, resource allocation to and within professions is partly based on criteria other than those grounded in the professional ideology of meritocracy. For example, two of the principal factors positively related to academic salaries are seniority and (male) gender (Konrad and Pfeffer, 1990; Bellas, 1994). A field's "feminization" is negatively related to salaries—the implications for student services, which employs relatively large numbers of women, are obvious. Similarly, one of the factors related to salaries and retrenchment is perceived ability to generate external revenues (Hackman, 1985; Slaughter, 1993). This may not bode well for student services, which focuses more on developing students than on generating external revenues.

The second dimension of place is horizontal, a continuum including the width/breadth of student services within colleges and universities and that extends to the for-profit sector. How secure is student services' place in higher education? In a time when colleges and universities are restructuring, who is getting cut? Higher education increasingly has come under fire for rising costs, declining quality of services, and inefficient use of resources. Thus, institutions have increasingly emphasized revenue generation, increased productivity and efficiency, and focusing the organization's resources on central functions and strengths. Such strategies generally call for some form of restructuring and involve downsizing some units and privatizing some activities. An orientation to productivity (cost efficiency and revenue generation) runs counter to the professional ideology of student affairs, which emphasizes service. New functions have emerged in colleges and universities, including offices designed to enhance institutional revenues. Accordingly, the conception of professionals is changing: emerging professions are oriented to generating new revenues; old ones are being transformed.

A third dimension of place is a combination of time, space, and shifts in the position of student services administrators and clients relative to one another. Throughout its history, student services' relationship to its clientele has changed. Relations are apparently changing again, with students cast in the role of consumer. Along with that has come an increased interest in cost and efficiency in the provision of services. To what extent does such a focus impact the way student services professionals are evaluated and the way in which they regard their clients?

Place in the Administrative Hierarchy

Student Services and Administrative Expenditure Increases. Student services increased its share of institutional expenditures in the 1980s, as did academic and institutional support. Moreover, expenditures on student services (and on academic and institutional support) increased faster (49 percent) than those on instruction (36.1 percent)—by contrast, operations and maintenance grew only 17.3 percent (Montgomery and Lewis, 1994). Yet student services is the smallest of four expenditure categories in administration, accounting for 16.8 percent of administrative expenditures in 1990, compared to 24.9 percent for the next smallest category.

Such figures belie accounts that lay the principal blame for increased administrative costs at the feet of student services. Nevertheless, expenditure increases for student services disproportionate to those for instruction is problematic at a time when colleges and universities are being criticized for not devoting more resources to undergraduate education. Just as academic units have been challenged to reassess their activities in order to cut costs and allocate more faculty resources to undergraduates, so administrative units are being challenged to reduce costs and improve efficiency and service to their clients. The reassessment of administrative activities and costs in student services should vary by institutional type, for there are different patterns of administrative expenditure increases by type of institution. From 1976–77 to 1990–91, student services' share of institutional expenditures relative to instruction increased in all institutional types: public universities, four-year, and two-year institutions, and private universities and four-year institutions (National Center on Educational Statistics [NCES], 1993, see Tables 331–335). Yet the shares of general administration expenditures increased faster than those for student services in all types of institutions except private four-year schools, where student services' share increased from 6.4 to 8.7 percent of institutional expenditures, and general administration's share increased from 20.4 to 22.2 percent (see also, Glasper, 1994). General administration's share increased the most in public two- and four-year schools respectively (from 18.1 to 21.6 percent and from 16.7 to 18.6 percent, compared to student services' share increases from 8.4 to 9.9. percent and 5.8 to 6.2 percent). The smallest increases were in public universities: student services' share declined, from 3.7 to 3.6 percent; general administration's share increased by just 0.7 percent; and general administration's share was the smallest of any institutional type (13.7 percent). In all institutional types (except private universities), the big loser of expenditure share was operations and maintenance (O and M).

Salaries of Student Services Versus Other Administrators. Another measure of standing in the administrative hierarchy is salaries. The National Center on Educational Statistics (NCES) data on median salaries of instructional staff and administrators in the 1960s and early 1970s enables comparisons within administration, and between it and faculty (unfortunately, the data is not broken out by institutional type). Between 1959–60 and 1973–74 salaries of deans of students, deans of admissions, and of registrars increased 117, 105, and 128 percent respectively. Such increases were greater than those for vice presidents and for deans of the college (95 and 105 percent), but less than increases for presidents, business managers, and directors of public relations, which increased 127, 146, and 143 percent respectively (NCES, 1980, see Table 101). The growth in the latter two positions is striking. Business managers' salaries started out lower than those of deans of students, and the salaries of directors of public relations started out lower than those of deans of admissions. By 1973–74, business managers' salaries were greater than the salaries of deans of students, and directors of public relations were paid about the same as deans of admissions. Given the explosion of growth in students, and presumably in the services they required, that is a surprising pattern. As numbers of students increased, students services' standing in the salary hierarchy declined.

As with total expenditures, growth in administrative salaries of student services officers in the 1960s generally outpaced growth in faculty salaries, which for all ranks combined increased by 114 percent. This growth is somewhat surprising given the demand for new faculty to teach the exploding numbers of students. A seller's market existed for instructional staff. There was a salary hierarchy in academe as well, by field and by rank: salary growth was greater for professors (118 percent) than for assistant professors (103 percent). But such increases for the most senior faculty still fell far short of increases for registrars, business managers, and directors of public relations.

For the 1970s and early 1980s, the pattern in salaries is similar within administration, but different for student services versus faculty. Administrators and faculty realized declines in average real salaries, but declines for faculty (16 percent) were greater than those for administrators (13.1 percent). Among administrative categories, student services fared the worst, with real salaries for job positions in this category declining 19 percent, compared to 12.7 percent for academic services and only 9.1 percent for business services (Hansen and Guidugli, 1990). The numbers vary for public and privates, but student services fared the worst. Overall, salaries in student services declined more than did faculty salaries (but not in public institutions). In absolute terms too, average salaries in student services were at the bottom of the administrative ladder. Again, the figures are surprising, for the 1970s and early 1980s were a time when services to students became particularly important in addressing the needs of changing populations of students.

Looking at just the 1980s, and just at the salaries of chief officers, student services is again at the bottom of the administrative hierarchy. In publics, the median salary for chief student affairs officer is slightly higher than that of chief development officer but lower than other senior officers—chief executive, chief academic, and chief business officers. In independent institutions, the median salary for chief student affairs officers is the lowest by more than $10,000. In publics, the increases in chief student affairs salaries are less than the increases of most academic deans (except arts and sciences, education, and fine arts): in absolute terms they are less than those of all but one academic dean (sciences). Surprisingly, in independents, increases in chief student affairs salaries are more than the increases of all academic deans except nursing and sciences: in absolute terms they are less than those of all academic deans except education, fine arts, and sciences.

Why might student affairs be in this position? The current political context and the relatively early professionalization of student services would lead one to expect the occupation to be higher in the salary hierarchy. One possible explanation emerges from research on the academic profession. Gender is among the most significant correlates of salary (Astin and Bayer, 1972; Bellas, 1994; Konrad and Pfeffer, 1990), and the proportion of women in a field is related to lower salaries (Fulton, 1975), holding constant factors such as labor market conditions, individual qualifications, and job characteristics (Bellas, 1994). Pfeffer and Davis-Blake (1987) found similar effects for selected administrative positions in higher education: the proportion of women in particular administrative posts is negatively related to salaries. Although no current national data indicates the proportion of women in student services relative to other branches of administration, at the upper administrative levels, the proportion of women is highest in student affairs (Touchton and Davis, 1991). Even in the late 1950s, women were far more highly represented in student services (44 percent) than in general administration (24 percent) (U.S. Department of Health, Education, and Welfare, 1962). Recent data suggest that numbers of women continue to increase in the field. For example, the proportion of heads of financial aid who are women increased from 40 percent in 1981 to 53 percent in 1987 (National Association of Student Financial Aid Administrators, 1989).

Positions in Student Services Versus Other Administrative Units. Another feature of stratification (that also contributes to administrative cost increases) is number of positions. However, national data on positions is aggregated into categories that cut across different branches of administration. From 1975–76 to 1983–84, the job categories that realized the smallest increases in numbers were service-maintenance workers (0 percent) and faculty (9 percent). Numbers of administrators increased 15 percent. The greatest increase (54 percent) was in nonfaculty professionals (Hansen and Guidugli, 1990). That trend continued through the 1980's, with increases in faculty, administrative, and nonfaculty professional positions being 9, 14, and 28 percent respectively from 1985–1990 (Grassmuck, 1990, 1991).

Containing Administrative Costs in Student Services. Despite student services' low place in the administrative hierarchy, its professionalization has been accompanied by increased functional specialization within student services, leading to an increased number of positions relative to faculty. Thus, some combination of increases in salaries and positions accounts for disproportionate increases in student services expenditures relative to instruction. Whatever the need for and quality of student services work, institutions of higher education—big and small—are looking for ways to contain costs. The principal expenditure item in such institutions is personnel—salaries and positions.

Some savings might accrue to institutions that limit salary increases of administrators to those received by faculty. Salary indexing among different branches of administration could reduce salary dispersion that is heightening the hierarchy in administration. A case can be made for student services in terms of internal and perhaps gender equity. Given the growth in administrators and nonfaculty professionals, two cost containment strategies make sense. To limit growth, positions in student services could be indexed against numbers of students or faculty. Moreover, administrators could reduce positions. In the short term, vacancies could be left unfilled. In the long run, the profession should rethink the extent of specialization and its effect on the interaction among units and on professionals' interaction with students.

Place in the Restructured Institution

Reorganizing and Reducing Administration. Most institutions of higher education are restructuring not just their academic programs but their administration. The American Council on Education's recent survey found that "Reorganization and redirection may be the defining themes of the 1990's for American higher education. Two-thirds of colleges and universities have taken action recently to reorganize their administrative operations" (El-Khawas, 1994, p.1). General administrative restructuring is characterized by two patterns. First, institutions are more likely to reorganize offices and activities than reduce administrative layers and positions. Nearly two-thirds of all institutions are reorganizing administrative offices, and well over half are redesigning administrative activity. About one-third are reducing administrative layers, 29 percent are reducing senior administrative positions, and 35 percent are reducing other administrative positions. (American Council on Education [ACE], 1994, see Table A7). A second pattern is that a substantial proportion of institutions are contracting out for various services, and are seeking to enhance revenues, particularly through established means such as fund raising but also through new revenue-producing uses of facilities. Close to 20 percent of all institutions are contracting for various services such as ground maintenance, safety, and security. About one-third are utilizing facilities in new revenue producing ways, and 80 percent are increasing their fund raising activities.

Patterns vary by institutional type. Publics are more likely than privates to reorganize structures and reduce positions. The institutions most likely to reorganize and redesign offices and activities are public research and doctoral universities (75 and 56 percent). Those most likely to reduce senior and other administrative positions are public (37 and 55 percent) and private (41 and 53 percent) research and doctoral universities. Private institutions are more likely to contract for various services. Public research and doctoral institutions are most likely to increase their fund raising activities (91 percent) (ACE, 1994, Table A8).

Restructuring Student Services. What is student services' place in restructured institutions? To what extent is it being cut, and to what extent are services being privatized? Some 53 percent of colleges and universities are reorganizing offices and functions in student services (ACE, 1994, Table A7). As in the general administrative restructuring, such a pattern is strongest (69 percent) in public research and doctoral universities, but it is found throughout higher education (ACE, 1994, see Table A8). Reorganization is also more common than reductions in personnel or work: a substantial minority of all institutions have reduced student service staff (21 percent), hours of service (14 percent) and other elements of service (16 percent). Such patterns are more evident in publics than in privates, and most evident in public research and doctoral universities (39, 33, and 28 percent respectively). As in general administration, the focus on generating revenues has led to a redefinition (through privatization) of services. Over one-third of all institutions (69 percent of public research and doctoral universities) have set fees for some services. In a pattern that has implications for student unions and residential dining facilities, 58 percent of all institutions have contracted for food service. Part of reorganization is reorientation, with services restructured to generate revenues.

Salaries and Positions in a Time of Restructuring. The ACE data are based on reports from institutions about their actions. National data on salaries and positions offer an interesting balance to this perspective, although the national data are for a time period three years prior to the ACE survey. The national data are not sufficiently disaggregated to enable analysis of whether student services is getting hit harder than some other branches of administration, but they point to a continued increase in administrative costs relative to instructional costs throughout the system. They also are suggestive regarding the place of student services in a restructured college or university.

National salary data do not indicate that expenditures for administration were reduced more than those for instruction during the period of fiscal stress. In fact, administrators gained relative to faculty between 1991 and 1992 (following a previous six years in which administrators' salary increases outpaced those of faculty). Average faculty salaries increased by 2.6 percent (virtually the same for all ranks)—a slight decline in constant dollars (Lee, 1994). Salaries for senior administrators increased by the same amount (2.6 percent) in public institutions and by considerably more (6 percent) in independents. In publics, salary increases of student affairs chiefs were less than other senior officers (1.7 percent) and less than average faculty increases; in independents, salary increases of student affairs chiefs were higher (6.2 percent) than all but business chiefs (7.6 percent) and much more than average faculty increases. Salary increases for selected support officers were slightly less (2.1) in public institutions but considerably more (3.9 percent) in independents.

The story regarding positions is somewhat different. Personnel cuts tend to hit the bottom of the occupational hierarchy the hardest. Numbers of faculty and executives declined slightly from 1989–1991 (0.7 and 1.1 percent); support/professional staff grew by 6.5 percent. Numbers of nonprofessional employees declined 1.2 percent at this same time: the biggest reductions were in skilled (3.8 percent) and service (3.2 percent) workers, with the latter being the only category in which more than 40 percent of all employees are minorities. As with expenditures, O and M is the one administrative category that has lost share of total institutional expenditures.

Centrality and Marginality in Restructured Institutions. Restructuring in higher education ostensibly is geared to reorienting institutions to better serve and educate students. Student services should be more central than ever, strengthening its place in the institution and its claim on resources (Hackman, 1985). Yet that has not happened in public four-year institutions, which confront the challenge of addressing the needs of new student populations. Nor has it happened in public research and doctoral universities, where the pressure to reorient to undergraduate education would appear to be the greatest.

Part of the explanation may lie in two other goals of restructuring—to increase efficiency by containing costs and to increase productivity through generating revenue. In the current context, ability to bring in external revenues takes precedence over providing services. In explaining resource allocation among academic units, connection to external resources (for example, grants and contracts, gifts), and the potential to generate external resources has been linked to the internal allocation of state resources (Hackman, 1985; Slaughter, 1993; Volk, 1994). Units that provide services internally and are not seen as having the potential to generate external monies may be devalued and even marginalized. For example, large undergraduate enrollments may not generate proportionate allocations of state monies (Volk, 1994). Financial hard times may lead to maintaining services with reduced resources or reducing services—doing more with less. Lower-level positions are more likely to be cut; service is one of the employee categories most likely to be cut. The incentive is to charge fees for services that formerly were free and to generate revenue by privatizing some services. Such incentives derive from market and managerial based emphases on entrepreneurialism and are as powerful in small privates and publics as in large ones. Moreover, privatization makes sense in a neoconservative political climate in which public entities are under fire. Private business is assumed to deliver services more efficiently. That assumption underlies cuts in operations and maintenance and does not bode well for student services.

Given the ambiguity of student services' place in restructured colleges and universities, or the pressure to turn services into revenue-generating operations, what role might student services managers play in restructuring processes and settings? Student services professionals should take the lead in opening higher education to new student populations. In the past, pressure existed to establish positions and offices designed to provide services to special populations. Current pressures are to streamline student services and reduce duplication of work by eliminating offices for minority groups and making every unit responsible for serving these students. Neither scenario transforms the core activities of student services or the campus as a whole. In times of growth, new units are added to the core; in times of financial difficulty, newer units are sacrificed to preserve the integrity of the core. Such cuts can mean reducing the diversity of personnel precisely when campuses wish to attract and graduate more diverse student populations. Chief student affairs officers should guard against that pattern. The further challenge facing student services professionals is to restructure the delivery of services in ways that will improve all students' experience of the institution and enhance the experience of new student populations. Smaller can mean better. Such actions require ongoing input and control by students in redesigning services. The ideal is to transform institutions' basic structures (in delivering instruction as well as in student services) more than to develop interventions that adapt new students to old institutional arrangements.

Student services leaders should safeguard the educational bottom line. Too often, demands for greater efficiency and new revenues make the budgetary bottom line the end rather than the means. Shifting from free to fee-based services and contracting activities out to private business ought to be evaluated in educational as well as economic terms.

Place in Relation to the Student

Past Changes in Student Services Practitioner-Student Relations. For most of higher education's history, the relationship between campus officials and students was *in loco parentis*. Embedded in court decisions, the doctrine of administrators as proxy parents accorded them extraordinary authority over students, along with responsibility for and control over various realms of student life (Szablewicz and Gibbs, 1987). In the 1960s, students were successful individually, collectively, and legally in challenging the *in loco parentis* doctrine. However, if students were no longer "children," they were defined as needing "development" through activities organized by professionals. *In loco parentis* was replaced by *in loco counseloris*, a shift that fit student services' professionalization. Despite a demographic profile that was maturing, and despite students' successful political activities (for example, anti-war protests), student affairs' knowledge base described students as being at immature levels of development and requiring professional intervention. Parental responsibility for children was replaced by professional responsibility for clients. In place of moral or physical controls were efforts to shape personal psycho-social development through programs and activities. Some have suggested that in recent years a form of *in loco parentis* is returning (Szablewicz and Gibbs, 1987) as courts hold colleges and universities liable for personal injuries to students. Such cases may foreshadow another transformation in the relationship between students and student services personnel. That change is consistent with the language of business ideology that is filtering into the academy.

TQM and Students as Customers. Although its use and utility in the business world is dated and debated, Total Quality Management (TQM) has been adopted in some form by hundreds of colleges and universities, small and large alike, although mainly in nonacademic units. Whatever one's views about TQM, it challenges organizations and personnel to change their conceptions of and interactions with their clients. Students are defined as customers who must be satisfied. That shifts the relationship from educational interaction (between expert and layperson) to economic exchange (between deliverer and purchaser of services). Accordingly, the central goal is not to educate or develop the student but to maximize economic return from the customer. But what customers are served? The impetus for TQM is often industry's discontent with higher education's inefficiency and with new employees' training. Student services leaders would do well to ensure that changes in service have more to do with addressing student demand for improved service than with realizing increased efficiency to please those for whom we produce graduates. Students may become as much a commodity to be processed and produced as they are customers to be pleased.

Charging Fees and Processing Students. A trend exists in student services and administration toward setting fees for formerly free services. Treating students as fee-paying consumers may lead professionals to treat them with more respect, but introducing commercial images of students may adversely affect the relationship between them and professionals. Making students customers distances them from professionals and minimizes institutional investment in them. Instead of seeking to engage and enhance the experience of the whole student in various intangible ways, the aim of student services could become increasing the efficiency of interactions with students and maximizing the benefit to the institution from such encounters. Increasing productivity can quickly translate into an easily quantifiable measure such as number of students served. The incentive is to see more students for less time, to increase the number of students using the service, and to reduce the amount of time spent with each student (another way of saying the interactions are more efficient). The pressure is to process students quickly; those units in which service providers spend much time with individual students are evaluated as inefficient. Increased efficiency does not mean increased effectiveness. One of the principal findings of the literature on college and students is that relationships on campus are contributors to student satisfaction and success (Pascarella and Terenzini, 1991). Currently, the push is toward brief, efficient encounters that do not engage students or promote relationships. A similar pattern is evident in private sector service industry, which shows a significant difference between relationship-oriented and encounter-oriented organizational systems (Gutek, in press).

Processing students runs counter to meeting current challenges confronting student services. One of the critical challenges is to foster campus environments in which students from various backgrounds are valued and can thrive. The test is not to assimilate new students into the existing community, but to transform those settings and build new, inclusive communities. Such community must be grounded in relationships. Focusing on efficiency and revenues will likely lead not to a rethinking of service but to its cheapening.

Reconceptualizing Professionalism and Service. Student services professionals can reposition themselves by reconceptualizing the roles of professionals and students. Some professions (social work, special education) and professional reformers have reduced the distance between themselves and clients by becoming their advocates and by according clients a major role in defining needs and shaping services (Hoffman, 1989). The reconceptualization is not an economic one grounded in business—as with customer—but a political one grounded in consumer and civil rights. Students become more than just customers who must be satisfied. They are consumers who have rights and who can evaluate and hold campuses accountable for fulfilling their obligations. Students also become partners in shaping the organizational structures and processes designed to serve them. Such a shift in orientation involves treating students as adults who themselves care for and participate in the control of universities and colleges rather than being wards or customers. The content and quality of service are defined at least in part by the served.

Such reconceptualization requires a 180-degree shift in orientation—from seeing students as needing to be helped, to needing students' help. A basic challenge arises to student services' knowledge base—which is grounded in developmental and cognitive psychology and which individualizes and depoliticizes the position and interests of students (Hirt, 1992). A reconceptualization would transform not just practitioners' workplace but their professional education, which would address the political interests and collective dimensions and dynamics of student populations and life.

Conclusion

The traditional student services model has been grounded in services provided by independent professionals to individual clients. But professionals are now employed in organizations managed by people outside the profession, and managers' interpretation of the organization's interests often come between professionals and clients in the name of improving efficiency or enhancing revenues. That tension exists as much on small college campuses struggling to make ends meet as it does on large university campuses (although most student services personnel, like most faculty and students, are found on medium to large campuses). As organizations become more privatized, tensions for professionals providing services are likely to be heightened (consider the position of physicians in health maintenance organizations). Professions should reconceptualize their position and their relations with clients, and professionals must act not just on their clients but on the organizations that push them to process as much as to serve their clients. In doing so professionals must work not just with individual clients within the organization but with groups of current clients and with communities of prospective clients outside the organization. Professionals must become activists within their organizations to mitigate the effects of privatization within, just as at the turn of the last century they emerged as activists working through the state to mitigate the excesses of capitalism. Part of the reconceptualization is a new view of clients, aligning with them to ensure that organizations serve clients' interests. Part of it also involves restructuring services in areas and delivery systems (with clients' help) to reduce administrative costs.

References

Astin, H., and Bayer, A. "Sex Discrimination in Academe." *Educational Record*, 1972, *53* (Spring), 101–118.

Bellas, M. "Comparable Worth in Academia: The Effects on Faculty Salaries of the Sex Composition and Labor-Market Conditions of Academic Disciplines." *American Sociological Review*, 1994, *59* (6), 807–821.

El-Khawas, E. *Campus Trends 1994*. Washington, D.C.: American Council on Education, 1994.

Fulton, O. "Rewards and Fairness: Academic Women in the United States." In M. Trow (ed.), *Teachers and Students*. New York: McGraw-Hill, 1975.

Glasper, R. "Rising Administrative Costs in Community Colleges." Presented at annual Higher Education meetings of the National Education Association, Albuquerque, N.M., Apr., 1994.

Grassmuck, K. "Throughout the 80s, Colleges Hired More Non-Teaching Staff than Other Employees." *Chronicle of Higher Education*, August 14, 1991, 22.

Grassmuck, K. "Big Increases in Academic Support Staff Prompt Growing Concerns on Campuses." *Chronicle of Higher Education*, March 28, 1990, 1, 32–33.

Gutek, B. *The Dynamics of Service Interactions: An Essay on Transactions Between Customers and Providers*. San Francisco: Jossey-Bass, in press.

Hackman, J. D. "Power and Centrality in the Allocation of Resources in Colleges and Universities." *Administrative Science Quarterly*, 1985, *30* (1), 61–77.

Hansen, W. L., and Guidugli, T. "Comparing Salary and Employment Gains for Higher Education Administrators and Faculty Members." *Journal of Higher Education*, 1990, *61* (2), 142–160.

Heinz, J., and Laumann, E. *Chicago Lawyers: The Social Structure of the Bar*. New York and Chicago: Russell Sage Foundation and American Bar Association, 1982.

Hirt, J. "Professionalism, Power, and Prestige: Ideology and Practice in Student Affairs." Unpublished doctoral dissertation, Center for the Study of Higher Education, University of Arizona, 1992.

Hoffman, L. *The Politics of Knowledge: Activist Movements in Medicine and Urban Planning*. Albany: State University of New York Press, 1989.

Konrad, A., and Pfeffer, J. "Do You Get What You Deserve?: Factors Affecting the Relationship Between Productivity and Pay." *Administrative Science Quarterly*, 1990, *35* (2), 258–285.

Larson, M. S. *The Rise of Professionalism: A Sociological Analysis*. Berkeley: University of California Press, 1977.

Lee, J. "Faculty Salaries, 1992–93." *National Education Association 1994 Almanac of Higher Education*, 1994, 7–24.

Montgomery, D., and Lewis, G. "Administrative Staff: Salaries and Issues." *National Education Association 1994 Almanac of Higher Education*, 1994, 123–149.

National Association of Student Financial Aid Administrators. *Survey of Minority Financial Aid Administrators: A Report by the NASFAA Minority Concerns Committee, 1988–89*. Washington, D.C.: National Association of Student Financial Aid Administrators, 1989.

National Center on Educational Statistics. *Digest of Education Statistics*. Washington, D.C.: U.S. Government Printing Office, 1993.

National Center on Educational Statistics. *Digest of Education Statistics*. Washington, D.C.: U.S. Government Printing Office, 1980.

Pascarella, E., and Terenzini, P. *How College Affects Students*. San Francisco: Jossey-Bass, 1991.

Pfeffer, J., and Davis-Blake, A. "The Effect of the Proportion of Women on Salaries: The Case of College Administrators." *Administrative Science Quarterly*, 1987, *32*, 1–24.

Rhoades, G. "Rising Administrative Costs in Instructional Units." *Thought and Action*, in press.

Slaughter, S. "Retrenchment in the 1980s: The Politics of Prestige and Gender." *Journal of Higher Education*, 1993, *64* (3), 250–282.

Slaughter, S. *The Higher Learning and High Technology: Dynamics of Higher Education Policy Formation.* Albany: State University of New York Press, 1990.

Slaughter, S., and Rhoades, G. "The Emergence of a Competitiveness Research and Development Policy Coalition and the Commercialization of Academic Science and Technology." Presented at the annual meetings of the Society for the Social Studies of Science, New Orleans, La., Oct., 1994.

Szablewicz, J., and Gibbs, A. "Colleges' Increasing Exposure to Liability: The New *In Loco Parentis.*" *Journal of Law and Education*, 1987, *16* (4), 453–465.

Touchton, J., and Davis, L. *Fact Book on Women in Higher Education.* New York: American Council on Education–Macmillan, 1991.

U.S. Department of Health, Education, and Welfare. *Statistics of Higher Education 1957–58: Faculty, Students, and Degrees.* U.S. Department of Health, Education, and Welfare, Washington, D.C.: U.S. Government Printing Office, 1962.

Volk, C. "Resource Allocation at a Public Research Institution." Presented at annual meetings of Association for the Study of Higher Education, Tucson, Ariz., Nov., 1994.

GARY RHOADES is associate professor in the Center for the Study of Higher Education at the University of Arizona.

As the financial picture for higher education continues to shift, colleges and universities need to develop new sources of funding if they are to sustain viable programs of student services.

Sources of Current and Future Funding

Stanley R. Levy

Student services and programs as we now know them were modest in their initial expression and design. As colleges and universities grew over the decades, the kind and quality of services and support systems for students also grew. Have these services grown beyond the capacity of institutions to afford them? If these are necessary functions, what are the potential sources for funding? Originally, services and support programs were funded from a mix of tuition, gifts, endowments, and legislative appropriations. The supply of resources is not without limit. Ethical considerations (as discussed by Schuh, for example) also prompt concern that services do not exceed the capacity of students to pay. Can the college sustain even the most essential programs and services for students?

Traditional Funding Sources

Traditional sources of funding for student services include:

Tuition: collected from students based on either a formula, the aggregate number of credit hours elected, or credit hour by credit hour.

General institutional funds: derived either from funds endowed for the general operations of the institution, or from overhead charges that the institution assesses and receives for research and other public service activities.

General tax revenues: originated with state government and appropriated to the institution or, in the case of those states providing general state aid, to independent, private colleges.

Designated sources of revenue: derived from specific institutional operations and dedicated or reserved primarily or solely for the purpose for which the funds were collected.

Subsidies frequently were provided from whatever source was in direct support of a particular institutional program or activity. For instance, general institutional resources were made available to the college housing program, which otherwise would be self-sustaining, to cover utility costs.

Funding for the Future: Major Sources

Institutions must be increasingly creative in identifying new sources of funding to maintain existing programs and services and to address new needs. Tuition still represents the most fundamental source of participant revenue for the college or university. Increasingly, tuition charges will focus on the direct instructional costs of the institution and those functions most closely linked, such as library support. Whether in a public two- or four-year college or an independent one, tuition will be the most visible source of revenue and the one likely to attract the most public attention. Widespread pressure exists to restrain tuition growth. As Blasdell, McPherson, and Schapiro (1993, p. 29) suggest, "These [public] institutions have instead become more reliant on state and local appropriations, while experiencing considerable increases in the role of net tuition revenues. Hence, net tuition revenues play a larger role in 1989 than in 1979 for all types of public institutions."

Supplementing tuition, legislative appropriations for public institutions will continue to increase, probably more moderately than in recent years. Financial discipline in determining the level of tuition will become the order of the day for fiscal planners. Colleges should avoid the roller coaster behavior of tuition charges of the last decade.

Academic budget planners are not accustomed to consultation with prime constituents, and students have little role, if any, in setting tuition. But in response to student and other pressures, many colleges have adopted a strategy of being more open about where tuition funds go and how a particular year's increase will be distributed. The consumer orientation of students and parents toward total college costs—which include tuition, room and board where applicable, books, and other fees—suggests that colleges need to be more open about tuition policies and practices. Legislative concerns in the public sector cannot be avoided either.

With consumer reaction to rising college costs, the residence hall system is an excellent example of the realities of funding student services. Residence halls are expected to cover all costs of their operation. Room and board charges fund the college housing program. For many institutions, keeping the cost of housing low has been a fundamental policy consideration. As Winston (1993, p. 265) notes, "the extended, fifty-year series on tuition, fees and room and board charges at Harvard, Yale, MIT, Wesleyan, and Williams shows that room and board charges have been virtually constant in real terms over that long span."

Institutional subsidies to the housing program often have been necessary to maintain this relatively constant cost of college attendance. Some subsidies are obvious, such as residence staff salaries as part of the dean of students' office budget. Others are more subtle, such as absorbing the legal and accounting overhead expenses within the overall college budget. If these formal institutional subsidies diminish or disappear completely, college housing operations will have to cover all direct operating costs, including legal fees, interest payments on debts, and administrative management directly related to the operation of the halls. Moreover, they could be expected to make a significant financial contribution to the overall operation of the institution. This contribution—an "overhead tax" to cover the costs of other institutional services—is common among midwestern and west-coast public colleges and universities.

Assessing general institutional costs against the housing program raises concerns about access. Changing the pricing structure for student housing could force some students to seek educational opportunities elsewhere. Further, one can argue that the residential aspects of the college community should not be viewed as an income generator. College housing should be viewed as a "cost center" that pays its own way and as a necessary element of the total educational experience on a residential college campus. The setting of housing rates can be open or closed to the community. No better method of engendering support and advocacy for the housing program exists than when housing management includes the residence halls' student government in the decision-making process. A budget committee of the student government; open forums in the halls, where pie charts and other symbolic representations are used to describe the fiscal realities and needs; inviting the college newspaper to do a story on residence hall rates; an open letter to students in the halls and to their parents describing the needs, priorities, and proposals—all of these techniques are useful. Shouldn't the students be able to decide whether there should be a 9, 14, 20, or 21 meal-a-week plan? Is it not appropriate to include students in the decisions on how and under what conditions they are to live? Student involvement also provides management with necessary and desirable feedback on the quality of programs and services.

Student involvement yields better insight about the program, timely responses to service delivery, identification of points of conflict, and a framework for determining new needs and services. These same principles of involvement can be applied to other programs considered essential to the college community.

Fees for Service

Public colleges have long assessed a fee for some of the services and programs they provide. As Mills and Barr (1990, p. 24) suggest, "This approach to funding has emerged in response to the need for increased revenue and a philosophy that users of a service should pay the entire cost for that service. . . . As part of a budget support strategy, charging fees for specialized services can have merit."

A general student service fee assessed to cover the cost of the broad range of student services available on the campus is common. Services supported by student services fees can be divided into two distinct categories. Category one, mandatory student fees, includes areas where a specific good or service is provided for which there may not be any discretion on the part of the student as consumer. These fixed product fees relate specifically to an institutional service that may once have been funded by the institution's general fund. A transcript fee is one example. On many campuses the student health service is another. The second fee category is a fee for services that are necessary but not mandatory or obligatory. With these services or programs, students "vote with their feet." Examples include reading and study skills programs, on-campus copy services, student legal services, recreational programs and facilities, and the campus bus system. If the specific service provided is of a high quality and responds to needs of the individuals, then the service receives necessary and proper support. A basic premise to that which follows was well stated by Seymour (1994, p. 17) in his discussion of the core values of quality in the Baldridge awards: "The customer is the arbiter of quality. As such, customer-driven quality is a strategic concept. It is directed toward customer retention and demands constant sensitivity to emerging customer and market requirements." Where such quality of delivery of the product is lacking, students and others will publicly criticize the service and it will founder.

Fee-supported activities and programs lend themselves naturally to significant student involvement in the fee-setting and review processes. Extensive consultative practices ought to be the order of the day in initially setting the fee, but a more effective evaluative tool is available. Wise managers pay close attention to the revenue reports for projects, programs, and activities that are "fees for service." When revenues fall, good management explores why income has declined and adjusts the service to recapture the customer. This appraisal is especially noteworthy where the activity is discretionary. Students often focus on such fees as vehicles for exercising control or influence over the product or service delivered. In the college of the future, more direct charges for even the most basic student services will be assessed. Co-payments in student health care facilities are now frequent even where there is a mandatory fee for the service. For example, the student health service pharmacy generally requires at least a co-payment.

Fees for service often are truly "user fees." The persons paying the fee are those who directly and clearly benefit from the service, support, or activity provided. The program pays for itself, or at least is intended to pay for much if not all of its own costs, solely from the revenues received. Student orientation charges reflect one such example.

Mandatory Fees

No category of budget planning better lends itself to involving the student than mandatory fees. Students, as customer or consumer, should participate in setting fees with appropriate administrative officers. These same students will become advocates with the governing board, which will review the final proposals.

Given the need to tease out new sources of revenue, the tendency to move toward mandatory fees to support institutional programs will likely increase. With tuition associated with the central academic program, fees will be sought to cover an increasing array of student services. Counseling centers and health care systems, whether on a traditional basis or analogous to a health maintenance organization, are already widely supported by fees. Student activities have long been fee-supported. The future suggests that most other services, including career placement and planning units, general tutoring services and programs, and general student administrative services, will be funded by fees. As campuses continue to provide sites for easy student access to computers, much of this new technology will be funded by fees.

The experiences of a few college campuses point to another mandatory fee. Capital construction for classrooms and student support services will be repaid from student fees. A "bond redemption" fee may serve that purpose. Whereas historically the debt service obligation for a facility was assigned to the specific entity benefiting from the public borrowing—for instance an events building or recreation center—a generalized bond redemption fee spreads the cost across the entire student community. Unless prohibited by state law, a mandatory fee to cover the costs of the entire student affairs program may arise. Such a posture removes some costs from competition with the overall instructional budget but may impact the overall cost of college attendance.

Mandatory fees fall into two categories: refundable and nonrefundable. A refundable fee is assessed when the good, program, or service that is provided is clearly an option to the student. The fee is collected "up front," usually when tuition and other fees are billed. The student has the option and opportunity of obtaining a refund once that fee has been collected. One common example is the student activities fee. When the fee can be used to support controversial student programs or activities or to support a student legal service, some students will want a refund. The weight of legal opinion is that such refunds ought to be available to students under such circumstances. Usually, those who receive refunds are not permitted access to programs and services supported by the fee.

A nonrefundable mandatory fee is assessed against all students without regard to the student's academic standing, the level of the student's enrollment, or whether the student uses the service. Nonrefundable mandatory fees support activities, programs, or services considered essential by the institution. For policy, legal practices, or statutory reasons, these specific activities are not funded through tuition revenue. One common example of this type of fee is the charge to support the student health service. Even though not all students will use the student health service, the fee is assessed against all comers. More properly, these fees can be subsumed under the category of user fees but are distinguishable by the manner by which they are collected or assessed.

Refundable and nonrefundable mandatory fees lend themselves to considerable policy and program involvement by students. Which fees ought to be mandatory and which refundable? How often may the mix be changed and under what circumstances? Are they temporary or permanent? In some institutions, these fees are subject to reaffirmation by the student community in periodic open balloting. Such balloting ensures continuing student interest and justifies to governing boards and parents the continuing assessment of the fee.

Voluntary Fees

Voluntary fees are collected by the institution for specifically designated purposes for which there may be little or no institutional support. For example, voluntary fees may be used to support a social and community service program, an awards program, or the college newspaper. The voluntary nature of the fee allows each student to decide whether and how to provide support. These fees are comparable to the income tax checkoff in the public sector, by which a citizen may elect to make a contribution to a particular state or federal fund, program, or service.

Where such fees exist, institutional ground rules have been established about the continuation of the voluntary fee collection. Commonly, the institution may protect itself by charging the cost of collection against the fee. This approach ensures that highly problematic or controversial activities receive funding without necessarily making the college responsible in whole or part for the activity.

Funding for the Future: Other Resources

A major new source of revenue only recently explored by student affairs units in public institutions is private support. At the University of Illinois, the Luce Foundation provided substantial support for a program entitled "Take the Lead," a leadership development program for undergraduate students. Institutions such as Texas A & M, the University of Virginia, and the University of Illinois have actively sought the financial support of alumni and friends through annual giving campaigns and endowments. Such private giving goes well beyond student financial aid and may be directed toward any element of student affairs.

Annual giving campaigns frequently focus on alumni who were student leaders to support student life programs. Parent-targeted annual giving campaigns at public colleges as varied as the College of William and Mary and the University of Michigan have provided substantial support for essential academic programs and student programs. Student affairs offices also may find it desirable to identify staff and resources for future fund-raising purposes. Students can play a major role in such efforts in the assignment of priority goals for solicitation and in direct assistance in solicitation.

Sales of products can give institutions net gain and critically needed funding. Ice cream shops where there is a dairy science or dairy management program, farm products grown on campus to support student programs in the college of agriculture, or other products or services produced in laboratories or campus facilities associated with the athletic program contribute revenue that may benefit student activities. The presence on a campus of a hotel or conference facilities, where guest rooms and meeting facilities can be made available to the general public when not used for campus or college purposes, can be a potent source of revenue. When student residence halls are used for such purposes, room and board charges to students can be modified. When associated with a college student union, the net proceeds from hotel and conference enterprises can be co-mingled with the total operation of the student union and thereby support student programs. Much the same can be said for the net proceeds from campus bookstores associated with the student union. Concerts, plays, and activities of all sorts under the aegis of the student union can be subsidized by the net gain from such revenues.

Sale of goods and services to the general public by a college or university is an increasingly delicate issue. To what extent does the tax-exempt entity compete with local merchants who pay taxes? Policy issues surrounding these sales vary from community to community. Some states have taken action to control such activities, representing a very real challenge for the public college or university. The more closely allied the product, good, or service with the goals and the purposes of the institution, the more likely the college will be to overcome challenges to its retail sales activities.

In a practice primarily associated with athletics, colleges may license their logo, name, or other manifestations of the institution, the proceeds going to the operations of the college. Here, too, it is essential to keep in perspective that which is licensed and the entities or units that will benefit from the licensure arrangement. The athletic program may be the most common beneficiary, but agreements can benefit libraries, scholarship funds, and other institutional purposes. Recent soft drink and athletic shoe endorsements reflect this new source of revenue. Student needs can be addressed through such licensing arrangements, particularly when tied to student-oriented programs such as student-sponsored plays, musicals, and annual celebratory activities such as homecoming programs.

The role and responsibility for students in licensure is as consumer, not as policy planner or participant. To the extent that the college correctly identifies what students and the public at large are willing to purchase, licensing can be a successful and lucrative arrangement.

Patent revenues and income from faculty inventions do not ordinarily devolve directly to student services and programs. However, many colleges and universities distribute such funds on formula or petition basis across the campus. Student affairs ought to seek out such support. However, protecting the intellectual property of the college community is increasingly a priority.

Outsourcing is the final revenue generator in this category of resource development. Many colleges and universities have ceased delivering products or programs themselves. In return for a "consideration," usually in the form of a fixed or a guaranteed annual or biennial payment, a private sector organization provides the product, service, or support. Some historic student affairs programs lend themselves to being privatized: housing, food services, counseling services, health services, and career services. In the case of food services, leasing space in the student union for a private vendor is quite common. The vendor assumes responsibility for hiring, firing, and payment of employees, for the operation of the entirety, and for payment of taxes and other assessments for the activity. "The institution is still responsible, however, for providing a facility, monitoring the quality of the (food) program, and maintaining student satisfaction" (National Association of College and University Business Officers, 1992, p. 1209). Some of the liability and insurance costs, and some costs associated with the physical space, may remain with the institution.

Under such arrangements, students pay the vendor directly for the service. The college provides what is needed without having to take any financial risks or incur any formal responsibilities. The net payment from the vendor can as readily be assigned to support student programs as it can be assigned to general institutional operations.

The benefits of privatization vary. The motive should not be profit or a positive impact on the institution's overall operating budget. Instead, the purpose should be to provide better quality service. Privatizing ought to improve the institution's services—not be an avoidance of responsibility. Less clear in these arrangements is the structure for maintaining quality of service. When the vendor provides an essential service for large numbers of students or faculty, the institution should establish contractually a formal mechanism for customer and user concerns to be addressed by the vendor. Loss of control or influence over an essential product, good, or service can be quite harmful to the academic community.

As institutions expand on the goods and services for which they intend to make direct charges or assessments, one caution is necessary—do not cross the line where the good or service and the income derived violate ground rules of the Internal Revenue Service. Unrelated business income is subject to federal income taxes; institutions are no longer protected automatically when they undertake to provide goods, services, or commodities to the members of the academic community or to alumni (Noetzel and Hyatt, 1990). What the institution may say is related the federal government may not.

Design for the Future

The financial picture for colleges and universities is generally anything but bright. As Erekson (1986, p. 4) notes, "Financial decision makers in higher education are facing unsettling questions as they attempt to achieve financial stability for their institutions while maintaining vital academic programs. Financial concerns arise from uncertainties about all of the major sources of revenues for higher education."

"What is to be provided?" "Who shall pay?" and "How much?" are questions for which there are no easy answers. That which has been the usual and customary may very well change. The quality of the delivery of goods, services, and programs increasingly will be determined by what and how these items are provided or made available.

Financing student services has many possibilities. The influence of Total Quality Management principles suggests that the old adage "The customer is always right" may have found a new place within the educational community. In planning for the future, colleges need to consider the following:

What are the essential services and programs to be made available to the student community?

Having determined what is essential, how should these programs and services be funded?

What mechanisms need to be established, or enhanced, to provide timely and effective feedback on the quality of the service being provided?

How are the students' interests best represented?

What is to be done about programs and services no longer considered essential?

How does one manage in an environment that will likely shift and change?

What are the institutional and community implications of services and programs to be discontinued?

Responding to the above must be done within the context of a particular institution, its view of itself, and its mission. However, four basic questions apply without regard to the community context within which the decisions are being made.

1. Which goods, services, and programs are essential to the mission of the college? Many college services are beyond the scope of formal instruction. As important as the outcome of what to support, the process by which those determinations are made is essential.

2. How will the college provide for each service, and who will pay for it? The funding mechanisms noted above become particularly relevant. Those activities, programs, and services absolutely essential to the college's mission must be paid for from tuition revenues, legislative appropriations, and other basic institutional sources. Those viewed as not so intimately tied to the fundamental educational mission but still essential would lend themselves to mandatory fee status. Those that may be desirable but not essential would likely be user-fee supported. If truly needed, the service would survive; if it were serving no essential or useful purpose, it would wither from lack of resources and lack of support. The students would determine its acceptability and necessity.

3. Should the college itself provide the service or should it purchase the service from an outside vendor? The answer to this question is mission-related to institutional and service accessibility. In a large metropolitan area, the out-

sourcing of a product, good, or service might be much more realistic than in a smaller community where there is no natural, local, affordable vendor. An institutional service that is discontinued in favor of an outside vendor would be complicated and expensive to recreate. Thus the decision to "go outside" is one that needs to be taken with quite careful deliberation.

4. How does the college sustain the relevance of its services and programs? Student input is essential. The mode for providing such input will vary with the service and the program, but provisions have to be made for the service or program to continue as responsive and necessary to the needs of the community being served. Possible approaches are a quadrennial referendum; a joint student, faculty, and administrative board or committee to work with and advise the management; regular meetings with the relevant student governing or student representative group; or the use of continual surveys. These approaches may lend themselves to differential application even on the same campus. The crucial dimension is to tailor the input of the student customer to the service or program in a fashion that is most relevant and informative.

Conclusion

The funding predicament for higher education is real and not likely to turn for the better for some time. Student programs, services, and activities become vulnerable in tight budget climates as scarce institutional resources are directed to that which is perceived as central to the primary mission. Fees of one sort or another, new and unique sources of funds, and more effective use of what is available will have priority on the student affairs agenda. Central to the effort to generate funding will be the student's significant role as consumer, participant, and policy planner.

References

Blasdell, S. W., McPherson, M. S., and Schapiro, M. O. "Trends in Revenues and Expenditures in U.S. Higher Education: Where Does the Money Come From? Where Does it Go?" In M. S. McPherson, M. O. Schapiro, and G. C. Winston (eds.), *Paying the Piper: Productivity, Incentives, and Financing in U.S. Higher Education.* Ann Arbor: University of Michigan Press, 1993.

Erekson, O. H. "Revenue Sources in Higher Education: Trends and Analysis." In M. P. McKeown and K. Alexander (eds.), *Values in Conflict: Funding Priorities for Higher Education.* Cambridge, Mass.: Ballinger, 1986.

Mills, D. B., and Barr, M. J. "Private Versus Public Institutions: How Do Financial Issues Compare?" In J. H. Schuh (ed.), *Financial Management for Student Affairs Administrators.* Alexandria, Va.: American College Personnel Association, 1990.

National Association of College and University Business Officers. *College and University Business Administration.* Washington, D.C.: National Association of College and University Business Officers, 1992.

Noetzel, M. S., and Hyatt, J. "Auxiliary Enterprises: Running a Business Within an Institution." In J. H. Schuh (ed.), *Financial Management for Student Affairs Administrators.* Alexandria, Va.: American College Personnel Association, 1990.

Schuh, J. "Current Fiscal and Budgetary Perspectives." In J. H. Schuh (ed.), *Financial Management for Student Affairs Administrators*. Alexandria, Va.: American College Personnel Association, 1990.

Seymour, D. "The Baldridge Cometh," *Change*, 1994, *26* (1), 16–27.

Winston, G. C. "Total College Income: An Economic Overview of Williams College 1956–57 to 1986–87." In M. S. McPherson, M. O. Schapiro, and G. C. Winston (eds.), *Paying the Piper: Productivity, Incentives, and Financing in U.S. Higher Education*. Ann Arbor: University of Michigan Press, 1993.

STANLEY R. LEVY, currently adjunct professor of educational organization and leadership, College of Education, University of Illinois at Urbana-Champaign, served from 1979 to 1994 as vice chancellor for student affairs.

Good budgets flow from good planning, and good planning requires a careful process that asks the right questions.

Good Questions for Sound Decision Making

Thomas P. Boyle

In how many ways is your professional life becoming new and different? Restructuring and the accompanying declining resources are the fruit of increasingly rapid changes. The future belongs to those skilled in strategic exploration who can anticipate dramatic change and recognize the elements of such changes as the components of paradigm shifts (Barker, 1989). The ability to discern the right moment to move to a new paradigm may mean everything to your programs and campus (p. 89). This knowledge could be the difference between being handed a set of new rules and having the opportunity to write them. The current atmosphere may offer just such an opportunity.

Budgeting is a label applied to planning processes artificially set at one-year intervals. Although described and reviewed by researchers and writers in all possible fields, budgeting remains an inexact process. Good budget plans depend on good information; good information flows from asking good questions and understanding the answers. Good questions isolate important issues. Good questions must be the right questions. In elementary statistics we learn about Type I and Type II errors in hypothesis testing; however, consider Type III errors, which result when making decisions based on correct answers to wrong questions (Kirk and Miller, 1986).

Discovering the right questions to ask is a product of experience, campus traditions, organizational personality and vision, economic contexts, and the ability to anticipate events in the future. That discovery process is the focus of this discussion: a fresh look at the campus environment from a variety of perspectives, touching on the implications for the budgeting process in student affairs.

NEW DIRECTIONS FOR STUDENT SERVICES, no. 70, Summer 1995 © Jossey-Bass Publishers

In the face of restructuring, this chapter stresses the need to look at each unit's mission, vision, and values when creating a budget. Also, the environmental, organizational, and economic contexts of each institution must be examined before decisions are made.

Planning

Too often budgeting is seen simply as a numbers game—figures to be manipulated and totaled in a spreadsheet. Paradoxically, budgets are really not about numbers at all but are representations of a complex interweaving of constantly changing elements in the campus environment. Budgets flow naturally from good planning—good planning does not emanate from adequate budgets.

Deciding what to do flows from an understanding of who you are as an organizational entity on the campus. Who have you been in the past and who are you now? Is your self-image congruent with the opinion held by the faculty? Who does the senior administration of your campus think you are? Are organizational pressures changing you, and are those changes beyond your control? Whether or not you realize it, you and your programs have an administrative personality known in varying degrees around the campus. The higher the level of congruence between the way you see yourself and the ways in which the faculty, staff, and administrative offices on campus perceive you, the more readily your budget plan will find favor.

A companion question to "Who are you?" is "What do you do?" When was the last time you conducted any kind of an inventory of your programs and services? How many items in your portfolio consume resources and could easily (or painfully) be eliminated without serious degradation of service? Stated less strongly, think of better ways of doing what you do or consolidate elements of your program so you conclude with essentially the same services but with a dramatic reduction in the necessary effort.

The issues of who you are and what you do flow from where you want to be at the end of the budgeting period, which in turn is driven by where you want to be three to five years from now. If you have not given serious thought to such extended time frames, you are cheating yourself and your campus. For example, if your program provides services primarily for first-year students, you should know all you can about the eighth graders in your potential applicant pool. You also should have data on the current first-year students reaching back five years to build some demographic models of how the group is changing and how those trends should look in the future. There is no magic here, just prudent thinking about the populations you will be serving to inform your vision of the future.

Importance of Vision

Vision cannot be overemphasized. Envisioning the future allows us to become one of "those who do not accept current realities but see beyond them [and] become masters of change" (Conger, 1989, p. 37). The idea of strategic vision is not new and does not need to be defended here. For some, it is the "key to leadership" (Nanus, 1992, p. 3). Even King Solomon of ancient Israel stated, "where there is no vision, the people are unrestrained" (Proverbs 29:18).

The elements of good vision are conceptually simple, and yet at the same time extraordinarily complex as worked out in the life of the campus. A vision is, quite simply, a mental model of the future. But unlike other mental models (such as memories, fantasies, or daydreams) vision holds the power to transform an organization from the status quo into a future improved reality. Visions also tend to be idealistic in ways that can attract commitment and create inspiration. They fit the organization, clarify purpose, are easily understood, and are generally ambitious. A clearly articulated vision has a way of becoming a filter through which potential activities are screened and unrelated items eliminated. Visions focus the energies of the organization and eliminate or greatly reduce energy wasted on unrelated activities (Nanus, 1992, pp. 23–30). By this focusing process, the vision combats unhealthy control tendencies within many organizations (Kets de Vries and Miller, 1984, pp. 23–41).

However, a vision is not trying to be prophetic or control history. Nor is vision an organizational mission statement. Mission statements speak to activities and purpose; visions focus on direction. Remember, visions do not exist in reality, they are not facts, but rather are filled with assumptions and speculative judgments. A vision is neither true nor false, but only one of many possible futures; it is not set in stone, but is alive and subjectively adapted in the minds and hearts of the employees (Nanus, 1992).

A vision for a student affairs program would include students, staff, the campus, and the curriculum. It should be brief (no more than two sentences), inspiring, clearly stated in the active voice, reflecting on the present but focused in the future, setting high standards and idealistic in nature. Any budget planning activity that does not screen expenditure requests through the vision statement and evaluate such requests in light of how they advance the vision should be modified to reflect such connections. If you do not have such a statement, take the time to articulate one that connects who you are today with who you want to be in the future. Acknowledge "the first leadership competency is the management of attention through a set of intentions or a vision, not in a mystical or religious sense but in the sense of outcome, goal, or direction" (Bennis, 1991, p. 14).

Role of Values

Nanus, in a chapter called "Taking Stock: The Vision Audit" (1992, pp. 43–60), asks a key question. "What are the values and the organizational culture that govern behavior and decision making?" (p. 51). Notice the strong verb choice. He does not use "inform" nor even "guide," but rather "govern." The values of your campus and those of student services on your campus govern the decision-making processes. For your vision to have any chance of success, it must be consonant with larger campus values. These are not marketing or public relations values, but the real, actual or core values. You must be able to articulate core values of both the campus and student services. Those core values form the "lived ethic" of the campus and provide "criteria that legitimize institutions and roles" (Walton, 1988, p. 219). They are the elements "not manifest in paper and pencil responses to values inventories but in how we live our lives" (Bogue, 1994, p. xiv). Tools for conducting a "values audit" are available in the marketplace and can be considered (p. 90).

The vision should flow from the core values of your program, and any incongruity should be addressed. For example, if you are the new director of housing at a mid-sized state university but come from a small, residential, liberal arts college, your vision of housing for your new campus will have to undergo some adjustment. A large off-campus population is now a significant element, whereas before it was not a factor. Most areas of incongruity are more subtle than this example, but they will emerge during careful review.

Campus Environment

Significant research has been done on how to do environmental scans and is summarized well in other places. Most notably, you should consult the analysis by Kuh (1993) that reviews the importance of institutional context regarding student learning and covers a variety of key issues to think about in making assessments. Consider also Levine (1989), Schuh (1993), Barr and Golseth (1990), and Chickering and Reiser's (1993) discussion on creating educationally powerful environments. You may even have the inclination to delve into what some regard as apocryphal literature and look at Giamatti's (1988) conceptualization of the university, Hunter's (1991) treatment of the clash of cultures in this country, and most especially Schon's (1987) insightful discussion of the reflective practicum as a bridge between the learning environment of the campus and the working environments of the world. The purpose of this reading is to get clear in your mind what kind of organism a university is. Look for meaning, stretch for understanding, discover new questions, meet new people, think in new ways, and grasp firmly your own conceptualization of the campus with which you are comfortable.

One more resource is critical. Cohen and March (1986) present a very thoughtful and provocative discussion on the nature of the modern campus. They regard the university as unique among organizations. With the exception of teaching hospitals, these institutions are the single most complex organizations in which to work. They characterize the campus as an organized anarchy, a place with multiple loci of decision power, where goals are vague and often in constant flux, where technology is unclear (process elements often not understood), and where participation is routinely fluid. Intent and control are often impossible to determine when one examines outcomes from an external perspective (pp. 2–4). Their concluding chapter is devoted to a leadership paradigm that works within such a complex context (pp. 195–229). The campus tends to be a place where multiple decision processes and multiple leadership and organization paradigms are in effect, often within the same substructure. Intent and control are often difficult to discern from inside the organization as well.

Restructuring on the campus can be seen as simply applying new standards, as reactive problem solving, as forging new policy out of conflict, or as adapting what some other segment of the campus is doing. Decision models can be based on evolutionary design, rational choice, trial and error, bargaining and power, diffusion, or regeneration (Cohen and March, 1987, p. 276). However, getting reliable data on which to base a planning process is a difficult task requiring constant maintenance. The target is always moving and the reference points are always changing. The overlapping hierarchies that are constantly advancing and ebbing also serve as complicators in the task. Schon's (1987) primary thesis (echoed by Bogue, 1994) is that the professions need to develop artistic skills through reflective practice and thereby develop the constant internal feedback loops necessary to insure that ongoing personal growth remains a given. Those reflective, developmental (artistic) skills need to be brought to the fore in the preparation process for good budget planning. Maybe only through such reflection will you be able to see not only the need for restructuring, but key elements of the evolving rule changes.

A final point on the issue of the campus environment: the Internet is a rapidly emerging tool for data gathering that has no precedent in higher education with respect to availability, ease of operation, and the amount of data available. In the space of a few moments, you can be in the reference section of the Berkeley library, move to a discussion group on a topic of interest, access Census Bureau demographic data, and connect by electronic mail to acknowledged experts in a variety of areas. Answers to questions come from individuals on campuses as far away as Hong Kong or as close as the community college across town. Broad exposure to the professionally focused discussion groups on the Internet will increase your informational foundation. In thinking through the early stages of a budget planning process, you will find significant state and federal financial data online to save you time and energy.

Excellent resources can help you develop Internet expertise, even though the "'net" is still in the early stages of development as a layman's tool. Kroll's (1994) volume is already in the second edition, as is the one by Engst (1994). Both books are quite comprehensive and should answer most questions. Some resource guides provide listings of what is "out there," and Maxwell and Grycz (1994) provide a fairly comprehensive listing of available connecting points on the Internet. Any of these is a start, but they will not be very useful to you unless you sit down, log in, and start the learning curve.

Layered Hierarchies and Overlapping Contexts

One essential lens exists to look through when preparing for budget planning. Understanding the campus as an organized anarchy (Cohen and March, 1986) can be helpful in one sense, but self-defeating in another—much like swallowing the whole pie rather than snacking on a section at a time. In this context, there are three different (but related) ways to view the hierarchy of any campus, and a brief discussion is in order on the impact of relational matrices and power.

The first is to examine the cultural hierarchy of the campus. Schneider (1990, pp. 383–407) posits some key elements in his discussion of climate for service within organizations. In the same volume, Thompson and Luthans (1990, pp. 325–337) review ways in which dominant organizational culture is learned, fostered, transmitted, institutionalized, and (ultimately) changed within organizations. The key concept is that a vital link exists between culture and behavior (pp. 337–340).

Look carefully at important traditions, sacred values, historical roots, relative prominence of the campus in the community or city, and the dominant and significant minority cultures of the student body. From where does the driving energy of the campus come? What elements of process always go unchallenged? Is there respect, bordering on reverence, for certain traditions or rituals that are part of the life of the campus? You need to become a bit of an anthropologist to think carefully about the campus culture. This experience may be sobering because you may discover (as many have, often too late to matter), that student affairs is not thought of as an essential piece to the puzzle. Instead, your unit may be viewed as a detachable "add-on" from more generous financial times. Anticipating the impact of the cultural hierarchy on your budget request will enable you to develop a sounder strategy.

The second element, the political hierarchy, may be more obvious, but its impact is often more subtle. Wildavsky's (1988) reworking of his classic study offers advice on budgetary strategies for government agencies, and the first element is "be a good politician" (p. 101). People achieve significant political standing for a variety of reasons. They may be national figures in their respective disciplines or rising stars administratively with a broad mandate to "reinvent" the campus (and they may or may not have the organizational shrewdness to pull it off). They may have been in a key position (like campus budget officer) for many years and have detailed, intuitive knowledge of the system and where it can be massaged effectively to increase the likelihood of a positive response. They may be personnel officers who have done regular favors for the campus hierarchy and who have enormous influence.

The point is simple. Know who they are, how they can help you, and what their informational needs are. There is no cost to keep them advised on simple issues involving your program. There is no cost to invite them to key events where you can showcase your activity and even give them some form of honorary role. There is no cost to maintain their good will. The key political players on the campus often have never had involvement in student affairs. Until now, there may have been no impetus to educate them on who you are and what it is you do. Those days are past.

The organizational hierarchy is the third element in the mix. This element is easy because organizational charts tend to be published at least annually. Be cautious, for as Barr (1993) concludes, unique qualities of your institution are the most important elements in analyzing your campus organization. You should know who all the players are, who reports to whom, and how long they have been in place. Be able to speak intelligently to anyone outside of the institutional context about the functions of the campus. Be a student of your campus organization and know the details to a deep level. Know when people arrived, what schools they went to, and be on the inside of the relational matrices that are important for your program.

One element here is of paramount importance: know where the stress points are. These are where the organizational structure fails to function consistently and well, and where you need to spend extra effort in accomplishing important objectives for your programs. If you don't know of any on your campus, you have not looked carefully enough or you are part of a very small campus system. Stress points can work for or against you, and the choice is often yours to create. Energy and leadership are required to have them go in your favor, but the answer to the question of "Is it worth it?" is usually easy to move past.

The final element here is one of examining the relational matrices and power issues for your campus. A relational matrix can be defined as the people on the campus necessary to affirm a decision process. For example, suppose you, as a leader in student affairs, want to convert unexpended personnel dollars to equipment money and purchase replacement computers. You need the consent of the computer center director, personnel officer, budget officer, and dean of student affairs to accomplish this. Those four individuals plus yourself comprise the relational matrix for this decision. If your relationship with any of them is negative, your chance for a positive outcome drops.

In the organized anarchy (Cohen and March, 1986) that is the modern campus, your effectiveness is often based on your relationship with program areas that have nothing to do (organizationally speaking) with student affairs. Areas such as purchasing, accounting, plant operations, grounds maintenance, food service, campus security, budget planning, or athletics may not be part of student affairs, but during the course of a given fiscal period you will interface with these areas in ways either productive or counterproductive. Productive relationships require energy, personal investment, and an understanding that on virtually every important decision, the players that emerge as the decision coalition matrix will be unique. You need not be all things to all people, but you need to be a known quantity to them all. Doing so may help avoid the last-minute surprise that derails six months of planning.

The issue of power is always present. Fisher (1984) discusses power in the context of the modern university and provides a taxonomy that names the types of power and describes the usage of each, reviews the literature on power up to that point, and offers his insight as a former university president regarding what types work best in the context of the campus. Understanding the use of power is critical because of the many opportunities to use it well and further the goals of your programs. Though a bit dated, Fisher's treatment and insight is still worth a review.

A final point: these hierarchies and issues of power are always layered, and it is often hard to discern the key elements at a given moment. Regularly scheduled analytical reflection is critical to understand their interweaving. Answers often will flow readily if you ask the right questions. Discovering the right questions is even more important in the current context of restructuring, and the essential reflective time now takes on strategic importance.

Economic Context

Whether you are used to funding by a state, through student tuition, or indirectly from significant research dollars on your campus, the environment has changed. In the not-too-distant past, student affairs in the California State University was funded by a student services fee that automatically kept up with inflation. That fee became the university fee, and the monopoly disappeared. The end of the first fiscal quarter of a given year now often rolls around before a clear budget picture is available. No longer in possession of sole ownership of the primary income source, student affairs is in competition with the general campus for scarce dollars in a university system that, in turn, vies with other state operations. Reductions of 15 to 25 percent are not uncommon for student services programs on campuses. Declining resources is not a temporary departure from the growth of the last decades; it is the new norm. Your private and personal response should include two elements that will help you to be ready to take advantage of a change in circumstances.

The first element is learning some higher-level data manipulation skills with spreadsheet technology to build budgetary models that make sense to you. Any set of numbers can be loaded into a spreadsheet and manipulated in a variety of ways, each giving you another piece to the budget puzzle. Budget utilization trends, equipment maintenance costs, copier costs, enrollment numbers, yield of applications as they relate to costs expended for recruitment can be determined or even compared to the costs of service on a per student basis office to office. Never depend on only one set of numbers. The more information you can generate on your own for the leadership group in student affairs, the better positioned you will be to articulate the important issues and justify what you are doing.

For example, a continuing concern for many campuses is the level of minority student enrollment. Often very limited useable data exist on enrollment and persistence. Suppose you only had applicant pool data for minority enrollment in grade 5, grade 8, and at graduation for the past three years. Using that data, you can build a model on progress rates of potential minority students in the pool, learn if enrollment trends can be attributed to population increase or to efforts you had made, and determine where the most serious risk of attrition occurs and how much improvement was possible. That information could be a key element as you direct more effort and resources toward students at critical educational transition moments, rather than waiting until they are seniors.

Secondly, you need to become adept at anticipating best- and worst-case scenarios. This skill requires an intimate knowledge of the important details of program areas so you can talk about the impact of reductions or augmentations of program budgets. This examination is best performed in small groups of affected individuals, trading off the role of devil's advocate and thinking out loud about negative circumstances for the coming year. In this way, you are able to formulate intelligent responses in advance and reduce the prospect of major budget surprises. This process will deepen everyone's knowledge base on the priorities within student affairs.

Unforeseen Events

No event can be fully anticipated, but many can be predicted with a fair degree of accuracy. A few will come along and shock everyone. Think in terms of potential threats to your program's effectiveness. The goal is to reduce the major surprises to nearly zero and to have thought about those that may occur in a given fiscal period. In student services it is typical that 85 to 90 percent of resources are invested in personnel, so it is fair to assume that most of the events in this category will be sudden and dramatic personnel changes. Important people depart mid-year. The standard 30–60 day notice is no longer adequate, for in today's environment it is not unusual to take as long as a year to replace senior-level people. Some form of contingency planning is essential. Who is ready to move on? Who is likely to move on? Who would you like to move on? Who would be the most difficult to replace? Who carries with them a knowledge base that exists nowhere else in student affairs? These are questions that are easy to think of and are answerable if you force yourself to allow for adequate reflective time throughout the year.

The remaining elements consuming significant resources should be carefully reviewed at least annually outside the context of the budget preparation process. Student services programs are increasingly dependent on desktop computers and small local area networks of shared software within offices. These are expensive to maintain, but far more expensive to replace. Ask for a careful analysis of such systems each year separate from the actual budgeting process and base your decisions on current data, industry standards, life expectancy of the equipment, repairability, and other similar elements. Be able to ascertain the weakest link in the system up to the strongest, which will usually automatically prioritize where the funding is needed most for upgrades or replacement. Copiers, fax machines, scanners, and other ancillary electronic equipment should be viewed similarly.

Some events will blindside you totally, which cannot be helped. At those times, keeping your composure and perspective will be difficult. However, most events can and should be anticipated so that the impact on the program will be minimized and students will not even know a critical element of your program has been disrupted.

The Time to Make Decisions

There will come a time when you have enough information to make good decisions. You have to decide when that time is. You will never feel that you have enough information, and there will be in retrospect obvious elements you failed to see in time to respond well. The quantity of questions asked or amount of information you are able to assemble is not the focus. The key is asking the right questions. The process is qualitatively different for each campus environment and must be discovered through strategic reflection. In the context of restructuring, you should be prepared to articulate:

Who you are and what have you done historically.
Your core values.
Your vision for the future.
Your understanding of the campus environment.
An appreciation for the layered cultural, political, and organizational hierarchies of the campus.
The importance of key relationships (and where they are) on the campus.
A thoughtful analysis of the threats to your program.
The forms of power at your disposal that enhance your effectiveness.

Finding good answers to the right questions will insure that you will be ready for the most rigorous of budget processes, and that your work in student affairs will continue to be "a worthy way to spend a lifetime" (Rhatigan, 1994).

References

Barker, J. A. *Paradigms: The Business of Discovering the Future.* New York: HarperCollins, 1992.

Barr, M. J. "Organizational and Administrative Models." In M. J. Barr and associates, *New Futures for Student Affairs.* San Francisco: Jossey-Bass, 1993.

Barr, M. J., and Golseth, A. E. "Managing Change in a Paradoxical Environment." In M. J. Barr, M. L. Upcraft, and associates, *New Futures for Student Affairs.* San Francisco: Jossey-Bass, 1990.

Bennis, W. "Learning Some Basic Truisms About Leadership." *Phi Kappa Phi Journal,* 1991, Winter, 12–15.

Bogue, E. G. *Leadership by Design: Strengthening Integrity in Higher Education.* San Francisco: Jossey-Bass, 1994.

Chickering, A. W., and Reiser, L. *Education and Identity.* (2nd ed.) San Francisco: Jossey-Bass, 1993.

Cohen, M. D., and March, J. G. *Leadership and Ambiguity.* (2nd ed.) Boston: Harvard University Press, 1986.

Conger, J. A. *The Charismatic Leader.* San Francisco: Jossey-Bass, 1989.

Engst, A. C. *Internet Starter Kit.* (2nd ed.) Indianapolis, Ind.: Hayden Books, 1994.

Fisher, J. L. *Power of the Presidency.* New York: Macmillan and the American Council of Education, 1984.

Giamatti, A. B. *A Free and Ordered Space, The Real World of the University.* New York: W. W. Norton, 1988.

Hunter, J. D. *Culture Wars: The Struggle to Define America.* New York: HarperCollins, 1991.

Kets de Vries, M.F.R., and Miller, D. *The Neurotic Organization*. San Francisco: Jossey-Bass, 1984.

Kirk, J., and Miller, M. L. *Reliability and Validity in Qualitative Research*. Newbury Park, Calif.: Sage, 1986.

Kroll, E. *The Whole Internet User's Guide and Catalog*. (2nd ed.) Sebastopol, Calif.: O'Reilly and Associates, 1994.

Kuh, G. D. "Assessing Campus Environments." In M. J. Barr and associates, *Student Affairs Administration*. San Francisco: Jossey-Bass, 1993.

Levine, A. "Creating a Brighter Educational Future." In A. Levine and associates, *Shaping Higher Education's Future*. San Francisco: Jossey-Bass, 1989.

Maxwell, C., and Grycz, C. J. *Internet Yellow Pages*. (2nd ed.) Indianapolis, Ind.: New Riders, 1994.

Nanus, B. *Visionary Leadership*. San Francisco: Jossey-Bass, 1992.

Rhatigan, J. J. "Simple Gifts." Closing address at the National Association of Student Personnel Administrators annual conference, Dallas, Tex., Mar., 1994.

Schneider, B. "The Climate for Service: An Application for the Climate Construct." In B. Schneider (ed.), *Organizational Climate and Culture*. San Francisco: Jossey-Bass, 1990.

Schon, D. A. *Educating the Reflective Practitioner*. San Francisco: Jossey-Bass, 1987.

Schuh, J. H. "Fiscal Pressures on Higher Education and Student Affairs." In M. J. Barr and associates, *Student Affairs Administration*. San Francisco: Jossey-Bass, 1993.

Thompson, K. R., and Luthans, F. "Organizational Culture: A Behavioral Perspective." In B. Schneider (ed.), *Organizational Climate and Culture*. San Francisco: Jossey-Bass, 1990.

Walton, C. C. *The Moral Manager*. San Francisco: Jossey-Bass, 1988.

Wildavsky, A. *New Politics of the Budgetary Process*. Glenview, Ill.: Scott, Foresman, 1988.

THOMAS P. BOYLE is director of student life at California State University—Fresno.

Defining student services in educationally sound terms will ensure its future as a foremost institutional priority.

Criteria for Setting Allocation Priorities

James A. Gold

Decades of research point to the positive impact of student services on student development and learning (Pascarella and Terenzini, 1991), but student affairs does not enjoy a greater advantage in preserving its institutional resources given its high correlation with student satisfaction. Clearly a need exists to awaken educational planners to the upside potential for improving institutional effectiveness and student satisfaction by funding student services. Let us take this opportunity, under the cloud of austerity, to inform the entire campus community of our positive, documentable effect on the quality of student life as well as the direct or indirect effects on student learning. "In the cognitive realm, the percentage of expenditures invested in student services has indirect positive effects on degree completion and on all self-rated growth in leadership abilities, public speaking skills, and preparation for graduate school" (Astin, 1993, p. 330).

Strategic planning and setting priorities are a necessary part of the budget process. In cases of extreme financial hardship, retrenchment may be a necessity, but such action can be taken in a fashion that does as little damage as possible. Through the lens of the profession's literature, this chapter suggests standards and criteria for setting these priorities.

Prioritization Through Strategic Planning

Educational administrators cannot sidestep involvement with strategic planning and data management. "Colleges have no choice but to collect better information about themselves, their students, and what they are accomplishing—or failing to accomplish" (Keller, 1993, p. 11). The better prospect for student affairs administrators is to influence institutional strategic planning processes before the political and legal realities of threatened economic insolvency take over. "Reactive planning, the most usual variety, responds to the pressures of a changing world, political and/or economic environment, or value shifts. Proactive planning seeks to change things before there are pressures and problems—before the crises and before the damage" (Kaufman and Herman, 1991, p. 275).

Regardless of the unique campus character, subsystems, or priorities for student learning, the timing of planning is critical (Hull, 1992). "Planning is likely to be resisted and therefore ineffective if begun during a period of serious retrenchment" (Dooris and Lozier, 1990. p. 17). Positioning student learning and development priorities in front of campus administrators and governance structures while they are attempting to contain a forest fire of reactionary thinking will usually leave students shortchanged. The short-term realities of budget constraints flowing from enrollment decline or reduced funding can make idealized long-term strategic initiatives immaterial. If you can influence your campus today to make student learning the highest institutional budgetary priority, move ahead smartly.

Student affairs too often has been left out of institutional strategic planning processes. In crisis management, decisions are implemented immediately in the aggregate, leaving minimal room for adjustment to evolving circumstances. Emphasis is placed on the success and failure of the past, minimizing experimentation through visualization of an ideal educational institution. Decisions are framed in the present rather than toward the future. Analytical reasoning supersedes inductive thought and intuition. Predictability is valued above untested evolution.

Proactive planning for budget cuts and restructuring is always preferable to reactive decision making. The criteria are quite different. For example, strategic planning is value based and flows from the institutional mission statement, a document usually highly focused on student achievement. Regardless of one's theoretical perspective, the main reason goals are important is the clear evidence that people with goals perform at higher levels than people with unclear objectives. With proactive planning, the values, ideas, opinions, and even intuition of the planners are highly respected. Decisions are sequential and gradual, with examinations of the impact on the total learning environment. Total institutional effectiveness with student needs held preeminent becomes the principal determinant of structure.

Simulation of strategic alternatives should be brought into the campus planning process where practical facts of student enrollment and revenue sources can be matched with long-range strategic alternatives. Emphasis is placed on the contextual environment, including quality of life for students. Most acknowledge that change is impressible on all aspects of the institution, especially the students served. We join together through a conditional vision that is accommodative and inclusive. Immediate decisions can be framed by best-guess views of the future with emphasis on fluidity and creativity. The student personnel point of view stands the greatest chance of being decisively etched in the parchment of a formal budgetary strategic plan and serving to focus institutional consciousness during actual financial crisis.

Establishing Funding Priorities

The restructuring of a student affairs division must recognize the restructuring of power and power relationships in society at large (Abbasi and Hollman, 1993). In recent years, increasing job insecurity flows from a global restructuring of economies that clearly affects higher education. Public funding demands are escalating for all services. We have evolved from a society producing goods and materials to one providing services, from using product control methods to managing information technology, and from recordable units of production to procured image creation. During these changing times, sensitive appreciation of staff can set the stage for cost containment without disastrous morale problems.

Total Quality Management (TQM) principles are ideally suited to higher education with an emphasis on balancing expenditure control with the objective of a comprehensive learning experience for students. TQM puts the student buyer first. Accurate student retention analysis suggests that "College administrators and institutional researchers need to build a comprehensive, multiyear, longitudinal student data base that incorporates both student records and student survey data" (Wilcox, 1993, p. 36). Qualitative data must keep company with numbers in registering our ability to direct our funding priorities, particularly in matters of assessing the impact of reduced student services.

In the area of staff, the challenge will be to discover where budgetary change is possible, practical, and minimally disruptive to the institutional mission. Next, you must predict the likely consequences to student learning of cost containment or downsizing measures. Guidelines for action should include means for monitoring any problems resulting from priority shifts that occur when a plan is finally set in motion. As in weather forecasting, difficulty exists in accounting for all the variables that might influence your ultimate predictions. Regular monitoring is necessary. Establish functional priorities. Do an environmental scan. Create a structure for managing change. Create multifaceted communication systems. Announce your decisions sequentially. Implement described changes accurately. Solicit staff opinions and provide a timely system of appeals.

Not everyone will support your plan. The carriers of negativity in the organization will cause a reduction in productivity and an increase in feelings of staff helplessness. People may feel unrecognized, except in roles as troublemakers and complainers, and will leave the organization both literally and figuratively. Finding antidotes to learned negativity is much harder than avoiding careless procedures for restructuring and downsizing. Chief student affairs officers must be especially vigilant in reading their personal signs for "top-down" negativity. Rekindled enthusiasm for budget cutting may seem a terrible contradiction, but organizational renewal must be experienced as an energizing process of reanimation and healing, not one of sufferance and endurance. If negativity can be contagious, so can determination to implement change in an atmosphere that is invigorating and promising. Consider the following ideas for ensuring a high staff receptivity for change:

1. Offer a compelling vision of a promising future.
2. Use surveys, focus groups, and informal contact along with traditional meetings to brainstorm and problem solve; provide private time to deal with anxieties.
3. Enlist staff support and involvement at all phases of the cost containment and restructuring process, even if they beseech you to be exempted.
4. Communicate short- and long-term goals clearly through formal and informal means; state the importance to the success of the institution.
5. Prepare the community and the local media if appropriate.
6. Be actively visible, alert to feedback, and ready to clarify, reassure, and encourage staff. Recognize and respond to family concerns of staff.
7. Be vigilant in assessing all phases and aspects of the process and make appropriate adjustments, accommodations, and adaptations quickly.
8. Acknowledge problems and be open about the sincerity of your concern for staff welfare and security as well as work satisfaction.

Retrenchment as a Last Resort

Financial exigency propels some institutions to the brink of insolvency, and although salaries remain the most vexing of the escalating outlays in higher education, dreadful liabilities inevitably flow from the involuntary departure of loyal employees. Retrenchment, at times inevitable, should be avoided at all cost. The impact on staff morale and institutional reputation is frequently irreparable.

Collegiality and institutional allegiance are fragile qualities that can be destroyed in one ill-timed and possibly nonessential pronunciation of retrenchment. Internal communication about retrenchment must be extensive and wholly supportive (Schreiber, 1993). Some would credibly argue that retrenchment can be no less than a political maneuver designed to discriminate based on class and gender (Slaughter, 1993; Butterfield and Wolfe, 1993). One study demonstrated the disproportionately negative impact on minority students and faculty during these times of downsizing and limiting of enrollment (Morgan, 1993).

We work in apprehension as the popular press rails about inefficiencies in higher education (Farrell, 1993; Barrett and Greene, 1994). The widely read *Chronicle of Higher Education* describes the concomitant problem facing student affairs as academic administrators scramble to preserve threatened academic departments (Cage, 1992). For example, in response to the extraordinary budget cuts and escalating fee increases of the university and state university systems of California (68 percent in two years), campuses have protected academic and full-time faculty at the expense of other functions—especially student services. The learning needs of students have not been preeminent in this political process of infighting (McCurdy and Trombley, 1993).

Other alternatives must be exhausted before imposing economies gained at the expense of even one person's livelihood. Helpful guidelines exist for reducing costs and building in controls without eliminating staff (Hubbell and Dougherty, 1992). Ask first what can be gained by freezing or restricting equipment purchases, maintenance commitments, employee benefits, travel, professional dues and memberships, new hires (even emergency replacements), conference travel, and staff development activities. Additionally, ask what can be gained by encouraging staff leaves, closing down or selling facilities and other assets, creating early retirement incentives, raising fees, and developing new funding sources such as philanthropy. Perhaps there is wisdom in using across-the-board cuts to guarantee a semblance of equity at a time when infighting around survival issues threatens to wrench apart the fragile collegiality of higher education (Hartzog 1993). What may be seen as a coward's way out on one campus may be most prudent on another.

Standards and Criteria

An urgent need exists to state the case for the preservation and even expansion of student services at this time of great competition among colleges and universities. Because student services are demonstrably effective in retaining students, increasing their satisfaction, and promoting their growth and learning, promoting the continued well-being of our services is ethically necessary. In the following sections, three major documents defining our profession will be examined in the light of implications for making sound budget decisions.

CAS Standards. The *Standards and Guidelines* issued by the Council for the Advancement of Standards for Student Services/Development Programs (1986) is comprehensive for its clarity of program definition, including nineteen specialized student services. While the CAS standards were not expressly developed to steer budget cutting processes, they can serve the convoluted function of guiding the reversal or deviation of services during times of downsizing. The existence of these standards is a wake-up call to the profession to set benchmark guidelines for reviewing our offerings to students. They provide a rationale for the existence of our services in a superlative framework of model setting. They may increasingly be noticed by accrediting agencies familiar with the importance of standard setting in the approval of specialized academic programs. During the past decade, attempts have been made to create strong linkages between academic affairs and student services where intellectual and affective development of students is efficiently accomplished (Walsh, 1989; Turnbull, 1989).

A proactive approach to standard setting could forestall or minimize a "fair share" mentality for assigning budget cuts to the student affairs division. Because most student affairs units are small, the cut of even one staff member can reduce services substantially. Aggressively seeking compliance with the CAS standards at a time when the institution is not facing a funding crisis, such as during the annual budget building process, makes sense.

Regardless of the timing of the call to standards, we must be prepared to state criteria for measuring job effectiveness, including a behavioral statement of student outcomes. Unfortunately, many of us would rather live by our political wits than be called on to evaluate our program effectiveness. Perhaps the time has come when we must ethically require minimal compliance with some credible standards.

The self-assessment guides accompanying the CAS standards provide the perfect means to judge compliance with the overall document. "With the development of professional standards, student affairs staff have excellent tools to create, expand, explain, and defend important campus services and student development programs. The challenge for the student affairs professional continues to be the development and implementation of ways to use these standards in a coherent manner" (Bryon and Mullendore, 1993, pp. 513–514). The standards are coherent and comprehensible. Our own professionalism through compliance is necessary to give life to their sum and substance.

Student Learning Imperative. Traditional measures of institutional productivity just do not make the grade. Reducing the number of faculty and staff, putting a cap on salary increases, raising tuition, establishing institutional advancement offices, increasing faculty workload, or raising the state lotto allocation for education have contributed nothing to improved student learning. Paying attention to the learner (Johnstone, 1992) is the more appropriate productivity focus. The demonstrated mastery of knowledge and skills for the largest number of students over the shortest period of time provides an honorable and authoritative basis for judging the efficacy of higher education, specifically student affairs programs and services.

Philosophical shifts placing new emphasis on student learning and student satisfaction require that we state the criteria for setting funding priorities in a new language. The recently published Student Learning Imperative Project statement sponsored by the American College Personnel Association (1994) offers such criteria. As Calhoun states in the preamble: "The interval between the decay of the old and the formation of the new constitutes a period of transition which must always necessarily be one of uncertainty, confusion, error, and wild and fierce fanaticism."

Out of this uncertainty and controversy of priorities grows disenchantment with traditional institutional attributes and indices of success. Simply stated goals for student learning and personal development should replace the old criteria that essentially ignored the student. The public expects outcomes for students such as positive changes, employability, and adjustment to a rapidly changing economic and social order. These are our simple aims when we ponder our selection among thousands of higher educational institutions to pay tuition or make a gift.

The *Student Learning Imperative* can be reframed to provide a timely criterion for determining funding priorities and communicating the potency of student affairs services and programs' impact on student learning and development. As defined by the *Student Learning Imperative*, the learning-oriented student affairs division is defined by five overarching characteristics:

1. "The student affairs division mission complements the institution's mission, with the enhancement of student learning and personal development being the primary goal of student affairs programs and services." We are challenged to conceive and promulgate a student affairs division mission statement that asserts student learning and personal development as a principal purpose. Desired learning and personal development outcomes must be distinguished in the context of institutional values such as ethnic diversity, gender balance, equity, and justice. Historically, we have defined our services more in the context of the number of programs offered and students served. Our mission must now reflect specific, measurable learning objectives against which funding priorities may be adjusted.

2. "Resources are allocated to encourage student learning and personal development." Traditionally, student affairs staff may have unnecessarily limited the scope of their responsibilities to the affective aspects of learning and personal development. Our programming has been process rich and content sparse. Psychosocial models of student development have left knowledge acquisition and intellectual development to faculty. The student affairs staff of the future will require persons talented in expanded learning modalities, including intentional learning promotion affecting student behavior in a wide range of learning and personal development outcomes.

If student learning is to be the primary goal of student affairs, the talents of our staff must match or even supersede the ability of faculty to effect measurable learning objectives. Because of the reluctant credentialing of student affairs staff as educators, we must redouble our efforts to demonstrate measurable changes in students attributable to our individual efforts and collaborations with faculty.

3. "Student affairs professionals collaborate with institutional agents and agencies to promote student learning and personal development." The "functional silo" description of relatively autonomous and highly specialized student affairs units has historically prevented student affairs divisions from taking a holistic approach to student learning, even within the more manageable aspects of out-of-class learning. Making the myriad out-of-class experiences seamless for students will require a continuous interaction between student affairs departments and, even more dauntingly, an organizational objective that will require bridging the historical gap between adjacent academic units and the student affairs division. Collaborating within the campus as well as

connecting with community agencies, churches, museums, cultural centers, and schools will be necessary to make the student learning experience one of connectedness and full involvement.

4. "The division of student affairs includes staff who are experts on students, their environments, and teaching and learning processes." In an era which has seen the elimination or diminution of student affairs research arms, even while adopting performance norms and competency-based institutional learning goals (often imposed by state legislatures or encouraged by accrediting agencies), we must find efficient and valid means for learning about student performance. This includes defining our mission behaviorally, collecting verifiable learning outcome data, and managing the interpretation and application of the collected assessment knowledge. What are students doing with their time? How are they being affected by the complete institutional environment? In what ways are they accessing or ignoring institutional services, programs, events, and facilities? When information is available, who is using it, and in what specific way is the institution being recreated to support student learning?

5. "Student affairs policies and programs are based on promising practices from the research on student learning and institution-specific assessment data." What are the conditions under which student learning flourishes? Student affairs professionals will be increasingly challenged to learn how students learn and to acquire the skills necessary to participate in institutional assessment programs. Collaboratively designed and established assessment audits will replace the seat-of-the-pants approach to institutional reform that flourished during the decades of unrestricted funding and accelerated expansion of higher education in America. Shaping policies and practices within a student learning framework requires a substantial contingent of student affairs staff members to be competent in theory building and research on student learning and intellectual augmentation.

The time has come to invade faculty territory and respond to the call of the *Student Learning Imperative*. Just as "Presidents who emphasize structure and analysis may be seen by the faculty as insensitive to academic values and preoccupied with means rather than ends" (Birnbaum, 1992, p. 182), student affairs administrators need to find budget cutting strategies that are other than linear and adaptive. The art of leadership involves interpreting raw data, not promulgating it. An emphasis on survival with constant discussion of cutbacks is demoralizing and suggests that one is valueless in reviewing the purposes of a student affairs division. In a symbolic environment, the choice of words sets the tone for trust, cooperation, and collaboration in the forming of institutional priorities.

Perspective on Student Affairs. Marking the fiftieth anniversary of the 1937 *Student Personnel Point of View*, we have *A Perspective on Student Affairs* (National Association of Student Personnel Administrators [NASPA], 1987). Designed to stimulate an understanding of student affairs among leaders in higher education, this document provides an articulate statement on the expansion and changes taking place in student affairs over the past several decades. Because of its explicit declaration of assumptions and beliefs about higher education and the students served, the document contains important criteria against which decisions to cut budgets and downsize student services should be justified. Insofar as possible, the results of any budgetary cuts and reallocations should be examined against these criteria for enhancing core beliefs about our vocation. Listed below, these assumptions and beliefs depict the sum and substance of our profession:

1. The academic mission of the institution is preeminent.
2. Each student is unique.
3. Each person has worth and dignity.
4. Bigotry cannot be tolerated.
5. Feelings affect thinking and learning.
6. Student involvement enhances learning.
7. Personal circumstances affect learning.
8. Out-of-class environments affect learning.
9. A supportive and friendly community life helps students learn.
10. The freedom to doubt and question must be guaranteed.
11. Effective citizenship should be taught.
12. Students are responsible for their own lives.

"The beliefs and knowledge of student affairs staff influence the manner in which they work with individuals and groups, the ways in which policies are made, and the content of programs and services" (NASPA, 1987, p. 14). Questions need to be asked prior to and during the time that budget decisions are made. The following suggested questions are derived from the parallel expectations of student affairs staff found in *A Perspective on Student Affairs* (pp. 15–17):

Are the values, mission, and policies of the institution being supported?
Are the governance structures of the institution sharing responsibility for the decisions, and are students involved?
What will be the effect on the educational and social experiences of students?
Will the decisions jeopardize campus safety and security?
Will institutional values be enhanced by developing and enforcing behavioral standards for students?
Will student affairs staff be available to work with faculty in assisting student groups and individual students, including the encouragement of faculty-student interaction?
Who will advocate and help create an ethnically diverse and rich cultural environment?
Is there provision for handling student crises?
How will effective relationships with the community be developed and maintained?

Who will coordinate student affairs services and programs with the other major components of the institution?

Who will assist students in making the transition to college and to the world of work?

How will students manage their financial resources to enter college and graduate?

Who will help students to clarify values, develop friendships, and expand their aesthetic and cultural appreciation?

Will students be assisted in managing and resolving individual and group conflicts?

Will students be encouraged in healthy living and in confronting abusive leadership?

How will students come to understand and appreciate racial, ethnic, gender, and other differences?

Are there provision for students to clarify educational and career objectives and to explore options for further study?

What opportunities will exist for student leadership as well as recreation and leisure-time activities?

References

Abbasi, S. M., and Hollman, K. W. "Inability to Adapt: The Law of Managerial Ineptness." *Records Management Quarterly*, January 1993, 22–25.

American College Personnel Association. *Student Learning Imperative: Implications for Student Affairs*. Washington, D.C.: American College Personnel Association, 1994.

Astin, A. W. *What Matters in College? Four Critical Years Revisited*. San Francisco: Jossey-Bass, 1993.

Barrett, K., and Greene, R. "No One Runs the Place: The Sorry Mismanagement of America's Colleges and Universities." *Financial World*, March 15, 1994, 38–46.

Birnbaum, R. *How Colleges Work: The Cybernetics of Academic Organization and Leadership*. San Francisco: Jossey-Bass, 1988.

Bryon, W. A., and Mullendore, R. H. "Applying Professional Standards in Student Affairs." In M. J. Barr and associates, *The Handbook of Student Affairs Administration*. San Francisco: Jossey-Bass, 1993.

Butterfield, B., and Wolfe, S. "Downsizing Without Discriminating Against Minorities and Women." *CUPA Journal*, 1993, 44 (2), 23–27.

Cage, M. C. "To Shield Academic Programs from Cuts, Many Colleges Pare Student Services." *Chronicle of Higher Education*, November 18, 1992, 25–26.

Council for the Advancement of Standards for Student Services/Development Programs. *Council for the Advancement of Standards: Standards and Guidelines for Student Services/Development Programs*. College Park: University of Maryland, 1986.

Dooris, M. J., and Lozier, G. G. "Adapting Formal Planning Approaches: The Pennsylvania State University." In F. A. Schmidtlein and T. H. Milton (eds.), *Adapting Strategic Planning to Campus Realities*. New Directions for Institutional Research, no. 67. San Francisco: Jossey Bass, 1990.

Falk, D., and Miller, G. R. "How Do you Cut $45 Million from Your Institution's Budget? Use Processes and Ask Your Faculty." *Educational Record*, 1993, 74 (4), 32–38.

Farrell, C. "Time to Prune the Ivy: Soaring Costs and Cuts in Funds Mean Academe Must Restructure." *Business Week*, May 24, 1993, 112–113.

Hartzog, J. "Making the Hard Choices Fair Choices." *Academe*, 1993, 79 (4), 31–33.

Hubbell, L. L., and Dougherty, J. D. *Cost-Effective Control Systems for Colleges and Universities: A New Paradigm.* Washington, D.C.: National Association of Business Officers, 1992.

Hull, M. H. "University Planning and Budget Reductions." *Journal of Higher Education Management,* 1992, *8* (1), 13–18.

Johnstone, D. B. "Learning Productivity: A New Imperative for American Higher Education." *Studies in Public Higher Education,* no. 3. State University of New York, Office of the Chancellor, 1993.

Kaufman, R., and Herman, J. *Strategic Planning in Education: Rethinking, Restructuring, Revitalizing.* Lancaster, Pa.: Technomic, 1991.

Keller, G. "Strategic Planning and Management in a Competitive Environment." In R. H. Glover and M. V. Krotseng (eds.), *Developing Executive Information Systems for Higher Education.* New Directions for Institutional Research, no. 77. San Francisco: Jossey-Bass, 1993.

McCurdy, J., and Trombley, W. *On the Brink: The Impact of Budget Cuts on California's Public Universities.* San Jose: California Higher Education Policy Center, 1993.

Morgan, J. "New Study Portends Bad News for Minority Students and Faculty." *Black Issues in Higher Education,* 1993, *10* (12), 16–17.

National Association of Student Personnel Administrators. *A Perspective on Student Affairs: A Statement Issued on the 50th Anniversary of the Student Personnel Point of View.* Washington, D.C.: National Association of Student Personnel Administrators, 1987.

Pascarella, E. T., and Terenzini, P. T. *How College Affects Students: Findings and Insights from Twenty Years of Research.* San Francisco: Jossey-Bass, 1991.

Schreiber, W. "The Proof Is in the PR: Five Case Studies Offer Conclusive Evidence of the Value of Strategic Communications." *Currents,* 1993, *19* (9), 30–34.

Slaughter, S. "Retrenchment in the 1980s: The Politics of Prestige and Gender." *Journal of Higher Education,* 1993, *64* (3), 250–282.

Turnbull, S. *Services for Adult and Commuting Students.* Washington, D.C.: American Association of State Colleges and Universities, Tennessee State University, 1989.

Walsh, R. *Student Academic Services: Academic Affairs and Student Affairs Working Together for Student Development at Eastern New Mexico University.* Washington, D.C.: American Association of State Colleges and Universities, 1989.

Wilcox, J. "Delivering Executive Information Systems to the Executive's Desk." In R. H. Glover and M. V. Krotseng (eds.), *Developing Executive Information Systems for Higher Education.* New Directions for Institutional Research, no. 77. San Francisco: Jossey-Bass, 1993.

JAMES A. GOLD is associate professor of educational foundations at the State University of New York College, Buffalo.

Examining the ethical issues related to restructuring, this chapter iden-
tifies codes of ethics, discusses specific ethical dilemmas, and provides
recommendations.

Ethical Issues Related to Restructuring

Patricia L. Mielke, John H. Schuh

Inflation nibbles away at operating budgets and staff salaries. Unfunded federal mandates require that institutions provide a variety of services to persons with various disabilities and information (such as campus crime statistics) to all members of the campus community each year. State governments face increasing financial obligations because of the fundamental shift in their relationship with the federal government (Schuh, 1993). "Colleges and universities today face their most significant crisis in over 40 years. The analysis of this crisis has coalesced over the last year with a focus on the double-edged sword of costs: the expenses of institutions are too high for their revenues and the costs of what we offer are growing beyond students' (and their families') capacity or willingness to pay" (Guskin, 1994, p. 23).

The responses of institutions of higher education to these financial strains are tempered by their collegial nature and the traditional, shared decision-making process. Tenure and widespread consultations before major changes are made are two of many variables that make this environment different from the private sector. The decision-making process in an institution of higher education has been described by one author as "sometimes bruising" and "rough and tumble" (Moore, 1991, p. 2). In this environment, with resources in short supply and decision-making challenging, the student affairs officer (SAO) could be faced with having to reduce costs, restructure units, or reassign staff. These tasks should be undertaken using the most humane methods possible so the people affected do not have their lives torn apart. Having a firm set of ethical principles will help the SAO make the best choices from potentially unattractive alternatives. (In this chapter, SAO refers to department heads and mid-level or senior leaders who are responsible for

---

The statement of academic principles of responsibility appended to this chapter is reprinted, with permission, from Reynolds and Smith, 1990. Copyright 1990. American Council on Education.

making budgetary decisions that affect people and programs. Deans, associate vice presidents, and vice presidents or chancellors also fall under this definition.)

The literature of higher education is not particularly robust when it comes to providing guidance on the ethics of institutional operations. As May (1990) points out, "although colleges and universities are doing a great deal to address ethical issues in the professions and business, through courses, research and publications, very little of this attention has been focused on higher education itself" (p. 1). This chapter offers a framework for thinking about ethical principles through the use of codes of ethics and Kitchener's work on ethics in student affairs, identifies some of the unique ethical issues related to resource management, and discusses the critical ethical points in budgetary restructuring.

We do not pretend that making fundamental changes will be easy even with a firm set of ethical principles in place. We do believe, however, that the ethical principles advanced in this chapter will assist in providing an environment in which solid, careful decisions can be made with the least amount of disruption.

Framing a Discussion on Ethics in Student Affairs

The two largest professional organizations of SAO's are the American College Personnel Association (ACPA) and the National Association of Student Personnel Administrators (NASPA). As is a common practice for professional organizations (Stamatakos, 1981), each has adopted a statement of ethical principles designed to guide the practice of its members. Complementing these ethical codes is the work of Kitchener (1985), who developed a model of ethical decision-making in student affairs that has been widely discussed in student affairs literature. More recently, such documents as *Reasonable Expectations* (Kuh, Lyons, Miller, and Trow, 1994) have spoken to ethical issues on campus. For example, this document asserts that students expect their institution to model ethical and moral behavior in all transactions. These three references provide useful guidance for an SAO faced with difficult decisions related to budget and personnel.

ACPA and NASPA Codes. Regarding the financial responsibilities of members to their institutions, the ACPA code, a more lengthy statement of ethical principles than NASPA's, asserts: "[Members will r]ecognize their fiduciary responsibility to the institution. They will assure that funds for which they have oversight are expended following established procedures and in ways that optimize value, are accounted for properly, and contribute to the accomplishment of the institution's mission. They also will assure equipment, facilities, personnel, and other resources are used to promote the welfare of the institution and students" (1989, p. 9). This statement provides a useful overview of handling institutional resources but does not speak directly to circumstances in which budgets need to be reduced or staff reassigned.

NASPA's ethical statement also speaks to the fiduciary responsibilities of staff: "Members seek to advance the welfare of the employing institution through accountability for the proper use of institutional funds, personnel, equipment, and other resources. Members inform appropriate officials of conditions which may be potentially disruptive or damaging to the institution's mission, personnel and property" (1993, p. 15).

How helpful are ethical codes? Guy states that "Codes offer a touchstone for guidance and remind every employee to look beyond simple expediency" (1990, pp. 161–162). She adds: "Truly ethical behavior requires that one go beyond the bare minimum and act responsibly, with due regard to the well-being of society, the organization, and all its stakeholders" (p. 163). Starr agrees with Guy, concluding: "codes of ethics by themselves are not a panacea to insure honesty, integrity and ethical behavior in a given profession or industry; only the most naive individual could possibly think that" (quoted in McGee, 1992, p. 290).

NASPA's and ACPA's statements are similar in providing general guidance for managing resources. They do not address ethical responsibilities of members for the issues under discussion in this chapter. The SAO looking for more specific information will have to consider other materials beyond these two statements.

Kitchener's Ethical Decision-Making Model. Kitchener's work has been widely cited in discussions of professional ethics (Canon, 1989, 1993; Winston and Saunders, 1991). Although as Kitchener points out, "Ethical decision making is always a matter of a particular situation and that the facts of that situation dictate the ethical rules" (1985, p. 18), her work provides a general set of principles for student affairs work. Krager (1985, p. 33) used these principles to frame her discussion of administrative roles and resource management. Kitchener's principles and Krager's application of them to resource management include the following:

1. *Respect autonomy.* Individuals have the right to live as free agents. Krager explains that this principle is operationalized by allowing staff to express differing opinions, permitting staff to have discretion in managing resources, supporting each other's right to question the use of resources, and accepting the responsibility to express priorities in allocation of resources.

2. *Do no harm.* Clients or students should not be dealt a disservice by our interventions with them. For Krager, doing no harm means that resources are monitored and consultation is wide in decision making, funding is not the sole determinant in developing objectives, group pressure does not dictate resource allocation, and programs are discontinued rather than overloading staff with additional responsibilities.

3. *Benefit others.* Kitchener indicates that the health and well-being of others should be promoted actively. In resource management, Krager reports, inform staff of resource availability and limitations, seek outside funding, make managers responsible to divisional and student needs, and seek creative directions to accomplish goals with limited expense.

4. *Be just.* Kitchener defines this as not only distributing resources equitably but also treating individuals and groups fairly. Krager operationalizes

being just in resource management as adopting an equitable budgeting system and developing priorities based on institutional objectives, incorporating objective evaluation to help identify resource priorities, and being fair and reasonable in making demands on resources as well as in allocating them.

5. *Be faithful.* Among the elements of being faithful are loyalty, truthfulness, promise keeping, and respect. Krager advocates working to ensure that resource allocation is guided by institutional mission, goals, and objectives, honoring commitments to students and staff, honoring agreements with groups and individuals, and supporting espoused ideas and plans with adequate resources.

The reader is referred to Kitchener's work for a more complete discussion of these principles, which provide a widely adopted ethical framework for student affairs work (Canon, 1993). Another interesting framework for ethics in higher education was developed by Reynolds and Smith (1990). A chart of their academic principles of responsibility is included in this chapter. (See Appendix.)

Most of us draw on basic ethical principles, but many SAO's have not had formal coursework in the ethics of a particular function (such as budgeting and marketing). Furthermore, most of us who face serious restructuring decisions have few personal experiences or examples to draw on to help guide our decisions. We must remember that our general understanding of counseling ethics has provided a fundamental basis for our professional behavior. To this understanding we blend the obvious ethical considerations resulting from our role as public servants and fiduciaries. Finally, another set of ethical considerations should blend into our ethical behavior by virtue of the specific professional ethical guidelines or codes governing our business practices.

Ethics Related to Resources Allocation and Management

Most student affairs professionals are trained in basic ethical principles related to student personnel and counseling. Many of these principles are similar to Kitchener's and have general applicability to many ethical situations. However, some situations call for a more specialized form of ethical behavior that may be foreign to counseling and student affairs staff. For example, in the marketing area, are the products promoted in glossy publications and slick presentations being delivered as promised? In the budgeting area, does the budget reflect an organization's goals and priorities? These issues take the SAO into new areas and demand different approaches to ethics to help address administrative problems resulting from our roles as resource managers and supervisors.

Chambers enhances our understanding of ethics in higher education by acknowledging, "While there are universal statements of fundamental ethical principles which hold true in all settings, it is also accepted that they are notoriously useless in providing helpful guidance for practical problems[;] . . . there are a number of unique aspects of higher education administration which have ethical consequences going beyond the normal levels of socially accepted behavior" (1983, p. 2). This observation suggests that higher education administrators should remember that they are public servants who depend on the public's confidence and trust. "As with other institutions and systems that have far-reaching consequences for our welfare (e.g., government, health care, and business) we expect that colleges and universities will decide and act with fairness, cognizance of the consequences of their actions, and appropriate accountability" (Smith and Reynolds, 1990, p. 21).

Chambers explains why higher education is unique and why the public believes administrators have additional ethical considerations framing their actions and decisions. First, contrary to what legal advisors may suggest, the public believes higher education is still acting *in loco parentis.* Administrators work with young people who are in the process of developing cognitively and morally; consequently, we serve as powerful role models for our students. Second, colleges and universities historically are seen as autonomous in research and scholarship, as places where the nation's ideas develop. Federal, state, and local authorities therefore have shied away from intruding into academic matters. "No other profession save the ministry enjoys such autonomy in its practice" (Chambers, 1983, p. 35). The courts generally have accepted academic decisions at face value; in turn, colleges and universities must remain loyal to this public trust and confidence. Third, colleges and universities share a place in society with other groups as charitable enterprises and have a responsibility to act in society's best interest.

Institutions have increased in size and complexity, resulting in more difficult choices and decisions. "It is this very complexity, in fact, that has brought about ethical dilemmas and quandaries that, in simpler, flusher, and headier times, were problems which could easily be solved by money, fiat, by cautious invasion, or by outright disregard" (Baca, 1983, p. 8). Difficult choices regarding restructuring and fund allocations will arise more frequently in the future. Consequently, questions of morals and ethics will be raised regarding administrators' choices and decisions.

Critical Points in Organizational Restructuring

Three critical points emerge during a time of restructuring: consideration of options and alternatives, decision making, and implementation.

Consideration of Options and Alternatives. When considering the available options and alternatives that are possible through restructuring, utilizing the creative talents and imagination of many staff members may be useful. The SAO should present as much information as necessary and carefully listen to staff members' ideas. One recommendation is to spend a concentrated block of time presenting the immediate issues and answering any initial questions. After staff has had an opportunity to digest the information, they should have the opportunity to offer thoughts on where the organization is or is not working well, what improvements or efficiencies can be implemented, how the organization might be restructured, which are the least essential programs, and where budget cuts should be considered. Among these choices may be the privatization of services, implementation of an HMO or health care, or decentralizing career planning and placement. One ethical obligation the SAO needs to communicate effectively and reinforce throughout this process is that restructuring decisions will be consistent with the mission of the institution and the organization, not what might be most satisfactory to staff or those defending the status quo.

The advantages outweigh the disadvantages in such an open exercise. The biggest disadvantage certainly has to do with the time required to thoroughly educate staff about the complexities and nuances of the specific problems. However, staff cannot make helpful and substantive suggestions unless the SAO devotes the time necessary to educate staff members and answer their questions. Our experience suggests this time is well spent because by participating in the evaluation of the budgetary circumstances, staff are more likely to be invested in finding solutions rather than in resisting change. If the organization is generally viewed as collegial and professionally mature, this exercise should be helpful for both the staff and the SAO.

Such an exercise often involves significant learning on the part of staff in basic processes and principles of budgeting. Organizations that already have well-developed and broadly understood mission statements, and that have educated their staff on basic budget principles and practices, will be better prepared when faced with restructuring questions. If individuals are less experienced or there is some degree of paranoia among staff, this exercise could prove to be difficult and the information received could be viewed with a greater degree of skepticism. For example, if the SAO is new to the position, a sufficient level of trust may not exist between the staff and the SAO to allow for an open and honest dialogue. Additionally, if the organization has experienced a disruptive or turbulent period, perhaps with the previous SAO leaving under unpleasant circumstances, this exercise may serve only to raise staff's ill feelings and lack of security in their own positions. In such a situation, the strategy may have to be altered. However, basic ethical considerations should not be abandoned.

Several questions reflect the ethical dilemmas the SAO is likely to face during this phase. Should the SAO be completely honest and forthcoming about all the alternatives under consideration? If the SAO has made some preliminary decisions which will affect personnel, how much of this information should be shared and, if so, when? What is the right balance for concern for the individual versus concern for the organization? Is the SAO listening with integrity and being open minded?

Decision Making. The SAO is likely to begin this phase with decisions made in the context of broad objectives because specific details and dollar amounts are not yet available. The SAO can identify program areas and specific functions within each area where savings can be realized with the least disruption to the mission of the organization. As time passes, a more detailed plan will take shape and the SAO can make necessary specific decisions to achieve the required savings. Rarely do restructuring decisions become apparent at the same time that answers to projections and year-end closing are produced. A skilled SAO would be aware of such possibilities by at least the end of the first quarter of the fiscal year. For example, a housing director knows well before residence hall opening what the fiscal picture was at the prior year's closing and what the likely occupancy for fall semester will be. The general magnitude of the problem should be apparent at this time.

Savvy SAOs leave their options open as long as possible to take advantage of unforeseen circumstances. For example, some staff turnover will occur annually in large units, but predicting how many people will choose to leave at year's end is difficult until many months into a typical fiscal year. The SAO will want to use staff turnover to fiscal advantage and, in some cases, avoid actual staff layoffs. A decision made too early or late could drive away excellent staff because they will want to try to ensure their job and financial security. In addition, income projections could change with respect to items such as enrollment for the upcoming year or summer income, which could influence specific actions. Staff confusion and frustration are possible because staff naturally will press for precise answers early in the budget reduction process.

This time can be additionally confusing because the situation is rarely static. Variables change constantly in the life of an organization and a campus. For example, a state-assisted institution may experience budgetary cutbacks at the same time a student affairs department is experiencing separate fiscal problems. At some point in time, a decision may be made that departments or divisions will have to contribute or share in campus cuts. More and more, many of us (even those in auxiliary enterprises) have been mandated to contribute in alleviating a campus budgetary shortfall. When this situation arises, the severity of a budget crisis becomes more acute overnight.

Ethical questions at this phase are numerous. Are decisions communicated as compassionately and humanely as possible? Are they communicated in an open and honest manner? How much notice should the SAO give to specific staff in order to provide ample time for them to find new positions? Are decisions consistent with agreements and commitments made previously? Are promises kept? Are decisions consistent with marketing information? Are we delivering the products we sell? Do decisions reflect an emphasis on student learning? Will decisions truly promote the effectiveness of staff and the organization, or are they efforts to defend the status quo? Will decisions promote the racial, ethnic, and gender diversity among staff?

Implementation of Decisions. Implementing restructuring calls for integrity and efficiency. This phase can be the most stressful to the SAO who ensures that decisions have been implemented in the fashion they were intended. For example, the SAO responsible for making the final budget decisions may not directly supervise the staff slotted for layoffs but should be involved as directly as possible in the implementation phase to ensure the message is being communicated across all units as effectively and consistently as possible and that staff are being treated in a humane and caring fashion. Stress levels will likely rise because at this point decisions are actually put into action and the effects of staff leaving the organization due to layoffs or program cuts occur.

Not everyone in the organization will agree with or accept the SAO's decisions. Some will think the SAO did not go far enough in each of the phases, especially if final decisions affect staff personally, such as by being laid off. These individuals may need to share their personal perceptions of the decision-making process with others. The ethical dilemma for the SAO is knowing that inaccurate or distorted information may be discussed, raising the desire to set the record straight versus respecting a staff's right to confidential personnel decisions, their right to their own perceptions of the process, and their right to disagree.

SAOs are in a better position psychologically if they can accept that some degree of unhappiness is natural during this phase and not appear overly defensive. However, SAOs must be prepared to confront individual behavior when it becomes detrimental to the health of the organization. Several ethical questions face the SAO in this phase. When employee layoffs are necessary, is fair notice and full explanation of the decision given? How much responsibility does the organization accept in assisting employees in identifying their options and retooling them for future employment? Are decisions clearly communicated to students, staff, and faculty in a timely manner so reasonable decisions regarding their tenure with the program or organization can be made?

The professional who accepts a position as an SAO has one other ethical consideration. Prior to accepting a position as a department head, candidates are obligated to confirm that they will be up to the challenge of leading an organization through difficult budgetary times, that they will not defer decisions, and that they are willing to make tough choices. Ultimately, the SAO has the responsibility for making final budgetary decisions. The task becomes much more difficult when challenging decisions are required about employee layoffs, educational programs, or dedicating money to buildings or staff. We must accept our ethical responsibility as professionals with this understanding and commitment.

Other Ethical Issues Related to Restructuring

Several other issues need to be discussed briefly to present a more complete picture about the ethics of budget management and making difficult choices well. None of these topics is developed fully; rather, they are introduced as a means of stimulating further thought.

Cause and Effect. Brown (1992) refers to this dilemma as the "ethics of consequence" and observes: "Producing the most good and the least harm requires that we correctly estimate an act's or a policy's consequences" (p. 99). In cutting a budget or reassigning a staff person, the SAO must predict what will happen after making a decision resulting in change. Failure to predict results accurately has the potential to result in organizational turmoil, diminished staff morale, and perhaps most importantly, the intended consequences not occurring. For example, the potential savings of changing from a self-operated food service to a contract food service in student housing may be offset if students do not like the food and move off campus. If occupancy declines, the decision may actually cost money.

Pursuing Excellence While Caring for Others. Guy (1990) discusses a dilemma in which an organizational leader promised a promotion to a person but then received a directive requiring a much stronger, more experienced person in the position. Does the leader sacrifice the needs of the organization for those of the employee, or sacrifice the employee in the name of organizational efficiency? Similarly, if an SAO is forced to reduce a budget by 10 percent and has a unit that has outlived its usefulness but the staff are extremely loyal and have given years of service, is that unit eliminated? Many campuses dedicated large units to meeting the needs of students who were veterans of military service in the early 1970s, but with fewer persons serving in the armed forces, that need for veterans' services has been reduced. Are the staff in veterans' affairs offices eliminated when it is time to make budget reductions? Are compromises possible?

Rights in the Workplace. Werhane (1992) and Maitland (1992) vigorously debate the rights of employees in the workplace. Werhane's position is that employees have the right to meaningful work and should be able to participate in managerial decisions. Maitland takes a different view, arguing that in a competitive labor market such standards as notice of layoff, due process over dismissal, and the like are "superfluous" (Maitland, 1992, p. 61). In the abstract, this position may seem a bit harsh, but how much notice should an employee have before being reassigned? What role should employees play in deciding how a budget reduction is to be implemented? Do staff have the right to participate in management decisions and, if so, to what extent? How does case law affect restructuring decisions?

Conclusion

Ethical guidelines help shape the decision-making process when restructuring occurs. Additionally, they inform colleagues in a general way how decisions will be made. However, superimposing a set of ethical guidelines in a time of crisis is akin to closing the barn door after the horse has escaped. Much discussion is needed to reach a set of principles that staff can agree with before the crisis occurs. Discussions about ethics should be an ongoing activity of departments and larger units within the student affairs division.

Budgetary restructuring and concomitant personnel decisions create a difficult working environment for student affairs administrators. No matter how well conceived a reduction plan is, how thoughtful and caring the administrators are in working with their staffs, or how much consultation is sought, people still will feel poorly treated. Staying true to our ethical principles will help us address these challenges.

Appendix: Academic Principles of Responsibility

Personal Principles

Everyone in an academic community has responsibilities to:

1.1 demonstrate a respect for each person as an individual.

1.2 communicate honestly and truthfully with all persons.

1.3 enhance the self-esteem of other persons.

1.4 help build fair and compassionate social and cultural systems that promote the good of all persons.

Professional Principles

Professionals associated with a college or university have responsibilities to:

2.1 assist their institution to fulfill its educational mission.

2.2 strive to enhance the personal and intellectual development of other persons.

2.3 be compassionate, thorough, and fair in assessing the performance of students and professional associates.

2.4 exercise the authority of their office in ways that respect persons and avoid the abuse of power.

2.5 conduct their professional activities in ways that uphold or surpass the ideals of virtue and competence.

Systemic Principles

Colleges and universities have systemic responsibilities to:

3.1 be fair, keep agreements and promises, operate within the framework of the law, and extend due process to all persons.

3.2 strive for an efficient and effective management that enables the institutions to adapt to new opportunities.

3.3 be compassionate and humane in all relationships while protecting the safety of persons and property.

3.4 articulate their missions in ways that reflect their actual strengths and aspirations.

3.5 foster policies that build a community of racial and socioeconomic diversity.

3.6 assist members in their professional development while requiring competent performance from everyone.

3.7 support an internal polity that fosters and protects academic freedom.

Public Principles

Colleges and universities have public responsibilities to:

4.1 serve as examples in our public life of open institutions where truthful communications are required.

4.2 preserve human wisdom while conducting research to create new forms of knowledge.

4.3 serve the public interest in ways compatible with being an academic institutions.

4.4 enhance the development of international understanding and support the world community of scholars.

4.5 promote a critical appreciation of the creative activity of the human imagination.

4.6 interpret academic values to their constituencies.

Political Principles

Colleges and universities have political responsibilities to:

5.1 promote forms of polity based on an equal respect for persons.

5.2 foster policies that increase access to higher education for the poor, minorities, and other underserved populations.

5.3 help develop fair and compassionate means of resolving conflict between persons, groups, and nations.

5.4 nurture a community or responsibility that is sensitive to the needs of future generations.

5.5 be good corporate citizens in all external relations.

References

American College Personnel Association. *A Statement of Ethical Principles and Standards.* Alexandria, Va.: American College Personnel Association, 1989.

Baca, M. C. "The Right and the Good." In M. C. Baca and R. H. Stein (eds.), *Ethical Principles, Practices, and Problems in Higher Education.* Springfield, Ill.: Thomas, 1983.

Brown, M. T. *Working Ethics.* San Francisco: Jossey-Bass, 1990.

Canon, H. J. "Guiding Principles and Standards." In U. Delworth and G. R. Hanson (eds.), *Student Services: A Handbook for the Profession.* (2nd ed.) San Francisco: Jossey-Bass, 1989.

Canon, H. J. "Maintaining High Ethical Standards." In M. J. Barr and associates, *The Handbook of Student Affairs Administration.* San Francisco: Jossey-Bass, 1993.

Chambers, C. M. "The Social Contract Nature of Academic Freedom." In M. C. Baca and R. H. Stein (eds.), *Ethical Principles, Practices, and Problems in Higher Education.* Springfield, Ill.: Thomas, 1983.

Guskin, A. E. "Reducing Student Costs and Enhancing Student Learning, Part I: Restructuring the Administration." *Change,* 1994, *26* (4), 23–29.

Guy, M. E. *Ethical Decision Making in Everyday Work Situations.* New York: Quorum Books, 1990.

Kitchener, K. S. "Ethical Principles and Ethical Decisions in Student Affairs." In H. J. Canon and R. D. Brown (eds.), *Applied Ethics in Student Services.* New Directions for Student Services, no. 30. San Francisco: Jossey-Bass, 1985.

Krager, L. "A New Model for Defining Ethical Behavior." In H. J. Canon and R. D. Brown (eds.), *Applied Ethics in Student Services.* New Directions for Student Services, no. 30. San Francisco: Jossey-Bass, 1985.

Kuh, G., Lyons, J., Miller, T., and Trow, J. *Reasonable Expectations: A NASPA Project.* National Association of Student Personnel Administrators, 1994.

Maitland, I. "Rights in the Workplace: A Nozickian Argument." In L. H. Newton and M. M. Ford (eds.), *Taking Sides: Clashing Views on Controversial Issues in Business Ethics and Society.* (2nd ed.) Guilford, Conn.: Dushkin, 1992.

May, W. W. "Introduction." In W. W. May (ed.), *Ethics and Higher Education*. New York: American Council on Education/MacMillan, 1990.

Moore, P. L. "Editor's Notes." In P. L. Moore (ed.), *Managing the Political Dimension of Student Affairs*. New Directions for Student Services, no. 55. San Francisco: Jossey-Bass, 1991.

National Association of Student Personnel Administrators. "Standards of Professional Practice." In *Member Handbook, 1993–1994*. Washington, D.C.: National Association of Student Personnel Administrators, 1993.

Reynolds, C. H., and Smith, D. C. "Academic Principles of Responsibility." In W. W. May (ed.), *Ethics and Higher Education*. New York: American Council on Education/MacMillan, 1990.

Ryan, L. V. "Codes of Ethics." In R. W. McGee (ed.), *Business Ethics and Common Sense*. Westport, Conn.: Quorum Books, 1992.

Schuh, J. H. "Fiscal Pressures on Higher Education and Student Affairs." In M. J. Barr and associates, *The Handbook of Student Affairs Administration*. San Francisco: Jossey-Bass, 1993.

Smith, D. C., and Reynolds, C. H. "Institutional Culture and Ethics." In W. W. May (ed.), *Ethics in Higher Education*. New York: American Council on Education/MacMillan, 1990.

Stamatakos, L. C. "Student Affairs Progress Toward Professionalism: Recommendations for Action, Part 2." *Journal of College Student Personnel*, 1981, 22 (3), 197–207.

Werhane, P. H. "Persons, Rights and Corporations." In L. H. Newton and M. M. Ford (eds.), *Taking Sides: Clashing Views on Controversial Issues in Business Ethics and Society*. (2nd ed.) Guilford, Conn.: Dushkin, 1992.

Winston, R. B., Jr., and Saunders, S. A. "Ethical Professional Practice in Student Affairs." In T. K. Miller and R.B. Winston Jr. (eds.), *Administration and Leadership in Student Affairs*. (2nd ed.) Muncie, Ind.: Accelerated Development, 1991.

PATRICIA L. MIELKE is director of resident life, University of Maryland–College Park, and a member of the Association of College and University Housing Officers–I (ACUHO–I) executive board.

JOHN H. SCHUH is associate vice president for student affairs, Wichita State University, and has served on the governing boards of NASPA, ACPA, and ACUHO–I.

This chapter presents strategies for improving management within student affairs divisions to produce a better environment for working, budgeting, and creating streamlined service.

Management Strategies as a Basis for Budgeting and Restructuring

Dennis L. Madson

People are attracted to student services because they want to work closely with students or make a difference in the lives of young adults. Their educational or work background often reflects an emphasis on human growth and integrated development of the mind, body, and spirit and an understanding of how young adults relate to peers, parents, teachers, and people in authority. These attributes, however, are not sufficient for overall effectiveness as a student affairs administrator.

The keys to overall success and effectiveness are *integrity* and *credibility*. Simply stated, integrity is "doing what you say you will do." Proper follow-through and follow-up are critical in developing trust, which is the cornerstone to all positive human relationships. Credibility is a complicated, multidimensional characteristic. In student affairs work it starts with expertise in a specific program area, such as residence life, counseling, or student activities. However, a narrowly defined expertise will not produce credibility within the typical higher education administrative structure. Without overall credibility, the impact of our work with and for students is diminished.

Some faculty members and administrators think of student affairs workers as "soft thinkers" working in a "soft area." To prove overall credibility, student affairs professionals must demonstrate strong management skills in planning, supervision, evaluation, and especially budgeting. Brilliant, impactful student program ideas can be ignored if presented without thoughtfully crafted management data—such as trends in the field, payback timelines, tie-ins to institutional goals, or cost-benefit analyses.

This chapter describes six strategies by which student affairs professionals can develop management credibility and create understanding and direct support for the goals, functions and operating approaches of our work. Although not guaranteed, appropriate budgeting support usually follows. The final section of the chapter presents the process used by Lewis and Clark College in an administrative restructuring project.

Publicize a Student Affairs Mission Statement or Credo

Student affairs professionals are educators as well as administrators and have a distinctive role in the higher education process. This role should be described in a written statement. A student affairs mission statement or credo must demonstrate that our work with students contributes directly and significantly to the institution's overall purpose: the education of students. Furthermore, such a statement should articulate the basic assumptions and values of our professional endeavors. A successful mission statement should build on values expressed in the cornerstone documents of our profession, namely "The Student Personnel Point of View" statements of 1937 and 1949 published by the American Council on Education (1989). The drafting team should review two additional resources. One is "Reasonable Expectations: Renewing the Educational Compact Between Institutions and Students" (Kuh, Lyons, Miller, and Trow, 1994), resulting from a project sponsored by the National Association of Student Personnel Administrators. The other is a chapter by Lyons (1990), "Examining the Validity of Basic Assumptions and Beliefs," in *New Futures for Student Affairs: Building a Vision for Professional Leadership and Practice*.

The process of developing this statement is an important part of its impact and acceptance. At Lewis and Clark College, this process began in a regular department heads' meeting, where the need for what became the Student Affairs Staff Credo was identified and discussed. A volunteer drafting committee worked for weeks, producing a draft that was reviewed by all student affairs department heads. The resulting version was sent to student and faculty leaders and to all student affairs staff. This step provided additional valuable comments and promoted investment in this project through active involvement. All input was responded to. The final product was framed and posted in student affairs offices and presented to the board of trustee's committee on student affairs. This brief credo (1994) is printed below.

Lewis and Clark College Student Affairs Staff Credo

Serving, Challenging, Guiding, Teaching.   As staff members we choose to serve this academic community for the mutual benefit of all:

- We will help students develop a strong sense of self, accept challenges, evaluate choices and make decisions.
- We will challenge students' beliefs in a caring and supportive way.
- We will hold students accountable for their actions.
- We will model acceptance, appreciation and understanding of that which is different.

- We will practice honesty, professional integrity and civil discourse.
- We will demonstrate respect for students and colleagues, and strive to be mutually supportive.
- We will promote the total development of the student: mind, body and spirit.
- We will encourage life-long growth and giving back to the greater community.

We seek to create a community that values truth, knowledge, authenticity and human dignity; which builds on the legacy and traditions of Lewis and Clark College and which looks ahead to the challenges of the future.

Articulate Overarching Program Development Objectives for all Student Affairs Units

The components of a student affairs or student services unit are broad and diverse on most campuses. Student affairs workers may include custodians, psychiatrists, uniformed campus safety officers, academic advisors, residence hall assistants, chaplains, and coaches. The overall success of such kaleido-scopic divisions is enhanced by publicizing specific principles or operating goals that each unit and worker is expected to follow. To be effective, the specific objectives must be reviewed and revised on a regular basis.

Examples of such overarching principles for a student affairs division are:

- All services and programs will be student centered.
- Administrative structure will emphasize streamlined, responsive, coordinated service.
- Initiative and creativity are valued and should be reinforced by linking responsibility, authority, and accountability at all levels of the organization.
- It is better to fund a limited number of quality service functions rather than many functions at mediocre levels.
- Professional development is an investment in the future success of the student affairs division.

A cornerstone of such principles is the direct service motto. At Lewis and Clark College the somewhat windy motto is, "When a student contacts a student affairs worker, *this is the last person or the next to last person* that the student will see before he or she receives the information, help, or service needed."

Participate in a Meaningful and Visible Manner with Faculty

Every campus community has members who think student affairs work is ancillary or peripheral. To compete successfully for increasingly limited resources, student affairs leaders must develop meaningful and visible partnerships with faculty. These partnerships are best based on an understanding of our contributions to the education and development of students. Thoughtful, coordinated participation must be well planned and implemented with integrity.

All colleges and universities have a vast number of committees, councils, and task forces. Student affairs must be represented on many of these groups. Volunteer to provide a member who can make a valuable contribution to the group, then select a representative with motivation and skills. Rotate participation on an annual basis as a planned part of your staff development effort. Require representatives to report back to other student affairs leaders as a matter of course.

When establishing committees or task forces to support specific student affairs needs, always have a clearly written charge and, whenever possible, include faculty, students, and staff in the group. Demonstrate organizational efficiency. Institutions of higher education are better at establishing committees than they are at abolishing unneeded committees. Consider a "working policy" in student affairs of never establishing a committee without ending the work of another committee for which the value and contribution has clearly declined.

Attend general faculty meetings, faculty senate meetings, and faculty workshops or retreats. Speak out on important student affairs issues when appropriate. These meetings are usually open to student affairs professional colleagues; you need not be an official member of the faculty. Participation, if only as active listening, is vital in building mutual understanding and support.

Encourage all student affairs staff members with faculty-level academic credentials to serve as academic advisors to a manageable number of students. This effort pays dividends in several ways, by providing valuable direct service and additional perspectives on students' academic experiences, and connecting student affairs professionals with faculty via advisor training and the development of an intimate knowledge of the curriculum.

Create occasions for person-to-person contact. This is how the strongest relationships are built. A "take a faculty member to lunch" (or breakfast or coffee) program among senior student affairs leaders is a reliable method to build understanding and support. One way to begin this process is to invite new tenured or tenure-track faculty members to a one-on-one contact with the senior student affairs officer during their first term at the institution.

Share knowledge about students. Student affairs professionals are experts on college students. We have information on student-body characteristics and demographics, knowledge and experience with learning styles, and firsthand observations of what motivates or hinders student success. This student growth and development expertise can be extremely useful to faculty and should be shared formally and informally. Try one-on-one consultations regarding students having academic difficulty, formal presentations at faculty retreats or advisor training sessions, and sharing observations about student learning at faculty meetings.

Demonstrate Strong Commitment to Basic Management Principles Throughout All Student Affairs Units

The most powerful way to develop credibility as an effective administrator and budget manager is to "walk the talk" in terms of understanding and utilizing proven management practices.

Planning. Each operating unit should be expected to record and present its prioritized goals on an annual basis. Progress toward meeting these goals should be reviewed every six months, with appropriate adjustments flowing from these reviews. Annual reports should be required of every student affairs unit.

Communication. Regular, well-designed staff meetings are a must. Meetings should be prescheduled throughout the year and have printed agendas, action logs (rather than detailed minutes), and designated blocks of time for open discussion of important issues. Except in times of crisis or emergency, these meetings should never last more than ninety minutes and should start and end on time. Paying attention to these time guidelines will bring rewards and a positive reputation to the team leader.

In a healthy organization, the distinction between lines of communication and lines of authority is understood. The former should be open, flexible, and freewheeling to promote initiative, creativity, and a clear picture of reality. No one should feel threatened or undercut when the custodian or psychiatrist talks with the vice president for student affairs about an idea or problem. Nevertheless, when it comes time to do business (set policy or allocate resources), the lines of authority must be respected and clearly followed.

Fiscal Accountability. Student affairs staff enjoy being held accountable for their work when program budget development is clearly linked with individual staff responsibility and authority. Such accountability is fostered by an administrative structure that clusters functionally related programs and services and emphasizes team management. An effective resource allocation process starts with an articulation of needs, continues with a respectful debate of priorities, impacts, and available funds, and concludes—after hearings, discussions, or negotiations—with a clear decision and agreement on expectations and resources.

Accountability is severely undermined if the sign-off authority of the budget manager is not religiously respected. The named budget manager must always be involved in the discussion, understanding, and sign-off of all budget revisions or adjustments, not only in budget development. Nothing will deflate morale faster than budget modification from on high without the knowledge and sign-off (and, if well-handled, support and approval) of the budget manager.

Staff Development. Do not tolerate incompetence; teach staff to be competent. Usually underfunded and sometimes even ignored is the management practice of ongoing staff education and development, including programs for front-line staff. Staff development opportunities include: a basic library of professional books and journals; support for membership in professional organizations; funding to attend professional workshops and conferences (opportunities that must be coordinated and include an expectation to report back to colleagues); on-campus speakers, convocations, seminar series, and workshops dealing with institutional matters and with personal issues such as financial planning, stress management, and wellness-fitness; pairing new staff with experienced mentors.

Recognition. Throughout higher education the value of rewards, incentives, and recognition is often forgotten or overlooked. A verbal thank-you or an informal note for a job well done is always appreciated and a motivator. Formal programs recognizing the distinguished service of a team or individual are important symbols of excellence. Outstanding service awards that carry specific rewards such as a cash bonus, a staff development opportunity, or new job-related equipment are especially appreciated.

No recognition motivated by honest appreciation is trite. During the author's tenure at the University of Massachusetts and at Lewis and Clark College, the student affairs divisions launched straightforward service recognition programs that were subsequently adopted by the entire institution. The idea is to express appreciation for length of service to each employee on the occasion of his or her fifth employment anniversary, or multiple of such (ten, fifteen, twenty years, and so on). Small, increasingly valuable gifts are presented to employees at a celebration ceremony or convocation. This program provides a systematic way for managers and colleagues to say thank you to long-term employees for their loyalty, continuity of service, and performance.

Finally, the importance of designating a portion of the annual salary increase pool for distribution on the basis of merit should not be overlooked. Doing this requires proper evaluation of work and specific judgments of the performance of individuals or teams, and this demands honest appraisals and documentation. To do otherwise can damage the morale of staff members who constantly go beyond expectations to contribute to the goals of the organization.

Use Systematic Evaluation and Research to Guide Work Decisions

Information is power. Data from carefully designed studies are extremely potent in the budgeting process. Successful student affairs divisions must produce, at least through partnerships, credible student life research data.

Such efforts can be low key and low cost. Trends in the use of counseling services, student participation over time in alcohol-free social events, or a comparison of financial aid support among peer institutions can be determined at minimal expense. Regularly scheduled, well-planned open forums with students, faculty, and staff are another high-impact, inexpensive tool for collecting useful data. Such forums should be jointly sponsored by the student government and campus administration.

Student affairs is under increasing pressure for evidence of measurable results, and our constituents ask about the added value of a higher education. Academic departments and institutional research staff are resources, but student affairs must take the lead in certain research: periodic, random sample surveys of student satisfaction with the total college experience; assessment of the campus climate; student retention trends; careers of alumni. Obviously, this research information must be presented to be considered, and it should be utilized in the decision-making process of the institution. Policy, procedure, and resource decisions should flow from a careful analysis of the data and from professional judgments we develop from concrete experience on a specific campus. If student affairs research is not shared with appropriate colleagues, is poorly presented, or is perceived as irrelevant, it will be ignored.

Use Performance Evaluations

Performance evaluation of student affairs workers and teams is a critical ingredient in the growth and health of the division. Sometimes these evaluations are taken lightly and all work is rated above average or outstanding. This is a damaging mistake. The purposes of performance evaluations must be understood and supported by every employee. They are: to take stock of progress toward individual and team goals; to record and discuss strengths and weaknesses, opportunities and barriers; to develop constructive ideas for continued success; to agree on necessary modifications of goals and future expectations.

Performance evaluations of individuals should begin with the worker and the supervisor independently recording a summary of the employee's efforts for the review period. The subsequent one-on-one conference should include a discussion of how the supervisor could provide greater assistance to the worker in meeting individual and team goals. Finally, the evaluation process must include a summary of mutually agreed on, measurable objectives for the future.

Team or unit evaluations should be based on a review of written prioritized goals. An outside reviewer may be useful as part of the process. The objective vision and creativity generated by these fresh looks is usually worth the required investment of time and money.

Speak Out and Tell Your Story

Student affairs professionals are trained as helping professionals, not public relations experts. To many the concept of public relations has a negative ring. Inherently, we want to be appreciated for our efforts and find it distasteful to "toot our own horn." We need to get beyond these feelings.

Our impact depends on widespread understanding and support for our goals, broad involvement in our specific work through partnerships with students and faculty, and recognition for the results of our labor. Similarly, our resource allocations depend in large measure on how widely we tell our story. People cannot support what they do not know.

Student affairs divisions should have a formal or informal public relations plan, which may include: an annual report that itemizes philosophy, accomplishments, and future plans; the development and engagement of the student affairs committee of the board of trustees; regular attendance of student affairs leaders at faculty and student government meetings, where they speak out on issues affecting students; advertised, systematic, informal contact with randomly selected students, for example, a "have lunch with the dean" program; featured student affairs articles in campus publications such as student newspapers and the alumni newsletter.

One College's Approach to Administrative Restructuring

Lewis and Clark is a medium-sized institution of higher education that includes an undergraduate liberal arts college (1,800 students), a law school (750 students), and a graduate school (700 students). Several years ago, President Michael Mooney began a project aimed at restructuring the administrative services. Three goals were identified for this project:

Development of coordinated, responsive (user friendly), efficient, and effective programs and services.
Promotion of staff initiative and creativity.
Streamlined and clear authority, responsibility, and accountability for all administrative functions.

The project approach assumed an open, flexible, progressive style of looking at management, not just a tinkering with the existing bureaucratic line structure. A management consultant, used sparingly, spent limited time on campus interviewing vice presidents, deans, and selected second-line leaders. This input resulted in a "Proposed Table of Responsibility-Centered Organization." The president conducted a series of two-hour meetings with the faculties of each school, the support staff, and the professional staff. These were designed to explain the project goals and the proposed organizational format and to seek ideas, suggestions, and support. Several weeks after these meetings concluded, President Mooney issued a statement, "Lewis and Clark College, Project 2000," outlining his vision for the institutional future.

Prior to the end of the 1993–1994 academic year, the president formed an Administrative Restructuring Transition Team (ARTT) and gave it the following charge:

• Review the Project 2000 statement and, mindful of its vision, articulate specific desired outcomes for administrative restructuring.
• Involve the campus community broadly in the discussion of restructuring

goals and of the specific options for grouping functionally related programs and services.

- Recommend specific groupings of programs and services to form functional work teams within the established organizational framework.
- Propose a time schedule for implementation.

The sixteen-member team included staff and faculty, all chosen with three criteria in mind: credibility—broad respect throughout the institution; conceptual skills—creative, progressive, and practical thinking; guts—the ability to do or recommend the "right thing" in spite of personal or professional pressures. Members were not chosen as representative of specific constituencies. The author, the vice president for student affairs, was asked to lead the team.

The ARTT first met in mid June 1994, and although the summer period was beginning, members agreed on a regular work schedule. Almost immediately, the need for a team-building workshop was identified. An organizational behavior expert was hired to conduct a five-hour workshop on teamwork, held the third week of July. Two significant products sprang from the workshop: a written definition of success for the team, and the operating expectations for the ARTT. The latter is a statement of mutual commitment among members and has served the team well:

ARTT Operating Expectations

- Schedule all meetings in advance, for a defined period of time. Distribute agenda and related handouts well in advance.
- Come to meetings prepared. Attendance should be regular, prompt, and for the entire meeting whenever possible. Follow through with individually assigned tasks.
- Adopt an attitude and behavior demonstrating "positive change is possible."
- Maintain professional integrity. Respect the difference between public and private conversation.
- Be willing to express ideas honestly, view things differently, and respect dissenting viewpoints.
- Make decisions by consensus if possible, voting if necessary. Written recommendations only with two-thirds majority of those in attendance. Minority opinions may be attached to recommendations.
- Be supportive of team members and decisions.
- Maintain confidentiality of the process, but make regular progress reports to the LC community.
- Philosophic discussions must lead to pragmatic decisions that are able to be implemented.
- Maintain dialogue with President Mooney as to team direction and productivity.

ARTT next undertook its charge to broadly involve the campus community in discussions of restructuring goals and specific options for functional
service groupings. Team members decided to try to talk to every staff member
at every level in each of the three schools. An approach was designed and
announced, the team divided into interview pairs, and small group meetings
began. The team asked several questions. With whom (offices/departments/
constituents) do you work most often, and on what concerns? What is going
well, what is not, and why? What are the most frequent concerns you hear
from students about your area and other areas? Do you have any suggestions
as to how communication among the staff could be improved? What else
would you like us to know?

Memos, e-mail, and oral suggestions were encouraged. Hundreds of hours
were spent collecting data, ideas, and concerns. Each duo listened actively and
carefully and then produced a written analytical summary and preliminary recommendations for their specific area. These reports were reviewed, starting
with those that promised to provide opportunities for the most impactful
change.

The team found that the majority of administrative hassles fell in three
areas: registrar, financial aid, and bursar. Furthermore, the current structure
contributed to these hassles: these three units reported to three different senior
officials, a dean and two vice presidents. Finally, they discovered technology
was not fully exploited in these areas. For example, financial aid monies were
not electronically transferred to the bursar's office.

The ARTT made periodic recommendations rather than a final, comprehensive report. The first recommendation was to bring the three identified
units together under one coordinator, with a strong emphasis on communication, cross-training, and accountability for student-centered service. This recommendation was implemented and the ARTT continued its work, focusing
on units including information technology, telecommunications, student life,
and athletics.

Perhaps the process will never really be complete, but the sun will set on
this ARTT effort at the end of this academic year, just a little over one year from
the start of the restructuring project. Throughout its work, ARTT has provided
progress reports to the campus community in the form of oral reports at faculty, staff, and student government meetings and written reports in the campus print media. Such update reporting is a necessary ingredient of any
successful restructuring effort.

References

Administrative Restructuring Transition Team. "ARTT Operating Expectations." Office of
the Vice President for Student Affairs, Lewis and Clark College, Portland, Oregon, 1994.
American Council on Education. "The Student Personnel Point of View, 1937." In *Points of
View*. Washington D.C.: National Association of Student Personnel Administrators, 1989.
(Originally published 1937.)

American Council on Education. "The Student Personnel Point of View, 1949." In *Points of View*. Washington D.C.: National Association of Student Personnel Administrators, 1989. (Originally published in 1949.)

Kuh, G., Lyons, J., Miller, T., and Trow, J.A. "Reasonable Expectations: Renewing the Educational Compact Between Institutions and Students." Unpublished paper, National Association of Student Personnel Administrators, Washington, D.C., 1994.

Lyons, J. W. "Examining the Validity of Basic Assumptions and Beliefs." In M. J. Barr and M. L. Upcraft, *New Futures for Student Affairs: Building a Vision for Professional Leadership and Practice*. San Francisco: Jossey-Bass, 1990.

Mooney, M. "Lewis and Clark College: Project 2000." Office of the President, Lewis and Clark College, Portland, Oregon, 1994.

Student Affairs Division. "Lewis and Clark College Student Affairs Staff Credo." Office of the Vice President for Student Affairs, Lewis and Clark College, Portland, Oregon, 1994.

DENNIS L. MADSON *is vice president for student affairs, Lewis and Clark College, Portland, Oregon.*

This annotated bibliography lists additional sources of information for understanding the current restructuring initiatives.

Annotated Bibliography

Dudley B. Woodard, Jr.

Higher education has undergone many reforms during the past one hundred years, but the current restructuring initiatives will likely lead to fundamental changes in revenue sources, incentives, and organizational structure. The following annotated bibliography will be useful to student services practitioners in understanding these changes and staying informed.

Annotated Bibliography

Association of Governing Boards of Universities and Colleges. *Ten Public Policy Issues for Higher Education in 1994.* AGB Public Policy Series, no. 94-1. Washington, D.C.: Association of Governing Boards of Colleges and Universities, 1994.
    AGB convened a group of higher education policy experts and asked them to respond to the most important national or state policy issues that will influence the future of higher education. This report summarizes the ten most important issues challenging higher education.

Association of Governing Boards of Universities and Colleges. *Trustees' Troubled Times in Higher Education.* Report of the Higher Education Issues Panel. Washington, D.C.: Association of Governing Boards of Colleges and Universities, 1992.
    This AGB report is based on a two-year study of the key trends that will shape our nation, people, and institutions. These data are then used to consider their influence on higher education and the resulting strategic issues for governing boards and institutions.

Barr, M. J., and Associates. *The Handbook of Student Affairs Administration*. San Francisco: Jossey-Bass, 1993.

Several chapters in this book address the administrative challenges for the future, including managing resources, budgeting and fiscal management, changing role of higher education, and fiscal pressures on higher education.

Breneman, D. W. *Higher Education: On a Collision Course with New Realities*. AGB Occasional Paper, no. 22. Washington, D.C.: Association of Governing Boards of Universities and Colleges, 1993.

This publication describes the financial problems facing higher education, a likely forecast, and possible responses to the new austerity of the future.

Breneman, D. W., Leslie, L. L., and Anderson, R. E. (eds.). *ASHE Reader on Finance in Higher Education*. Needham Heights, Mass.: Ginn Press, 1993.

This book describes public finance and financial management. The first section covers the fundamental issues in financing higher education, and the issues are explored through the analytical framework of public finance. The second section covers operational issues in higher education.

Bloland, P. A., Stamatakos, L. C., and Rogers, R. R. *Reform in Student Affairs: A Critique of Student Development*. Greensboro: University of North Carolina, Greensboro, 1994.

This monograph provides a critical, informed examination of the status of the student development movement. The analysis is helpful in terms of thinking about an alternative paradigm for student affairs.

El-Khawas, E. *Restructuring Initiatives in Public Higher Education: Institutional Responses to Financial Constraints*. Research Briefs, vol. 5, no.8. Washington, D.C.: American Council on Education, 1994.

A survey of colleges and universities was conducted to determine their responses to the financial constraints of the past several years. The report describes the types of actions and strategies undertaken to meet these financial pressures.

El-Khawas, E. *Campus Trends 1994: A Time of Redirection*. Higher Education Panel Report, no. 84. Washington, D.C.: American Council on Education, 1994.

This survey informs the reader of the trends taking place on campus and provides a context for thinking about educational reform.

Garland, P. H., and Grace, T. W. (eds). *New Perspectives for Student Affairs Professionals*. ASHE-ERIC Report, no. 7. Washington, D.C.: George Washington University, 1993.
This monograph addresses the changing conditions in higher education from the student affairs perspective and how student affairs can respond.

Layzell, D. T., and Lyddon, J. W. *Budgeting for Higher Education at the State Level*. ASHE-ERIC Report, no.4. Washington, D.C.: George Washington University, 1990.
The environmental factors framing state budgeting and how these factors affect state budgeting are discussed in this publication, which also discusses how the state higher education budget is linked to state objectives for higher education.

Pew Charitable Trusts. *Higher Education Roundtable Program: Policy Perspectives*. Philadelphia: Institute for Research on Higher Education.
These papers focus on timely issues challenging higher education.

Wildavsky, A. *The New Politics of the Budgetary Process*. (2nd ed.) New York: HarperCollins, 1992.
A classic book on the politics of the budgeting process.

DUDLEY B. WOODARD, JR., *is professor of higher education at the University of Arizona, Tucson. He was vice president of student affairs at SUNY–Binghamton and the University of Arizona and president of NASPA 1989–1990.*

INDEX

Ordering Information

NEW DIRECTIONS FOR STUDENT SERVICES is a series of paperback books that offers guidelines and programs for aiding students in their total development—emotional, social, and physical, as well as intellectual. Books in the series are published quarterly in spring, summer, fall, and winter and are available for purchase by subscription as well as by single copy.

SUBSCRIPTIONS for 1995 cost $48.00 for individuals (a savings of 25 percent over single-copy prices) and $64.00 for institutions, agencies, and libraries. Please do not send institutional checks for personal subscriptions. Standing orders are accepted.

SINGLE COPIES cost $16.95 plus shipping (see below) when payment accompanies order. California, New Jersey, New York, and Washington, D.C., residents please include appropriate sales tax. Canadian residents add GST and any local taxes. Billed orders will be charged shipping and handling. No billed shipments to post office boxes. Orders from outside the United States or Canada *must be prepaid* in U.S. dollars or charged to VISA, MasterCard, or American Express.

SHIPPING (SINGLE COPIES ONLY): one issue, add $3.50; two issues, add $4.50; three to four issues, add $5.50; five issues, add $6.50; six to eight issues, add $7.50; nine or more issues, add $8.50.

DISCOUNTS FOR QUANTITY ORDERS are available. Please write to the address below for information.

ALL ORDERS must include either the name of an individual or an official purchase order number. Please submit your order as follows:
Subscriptions: specify series and year subscription is to begin
Single copies: include individual title code (such as SS55)

MAIL ALL ORDERS TO:
Jossey-Bass Publishers
350 Sansome Street
San Francisco, California 94104-1342

FOR SUBSCRIPTION SALES OUTSIDE OF THE UNITED STATES, CONTACT:
any international subscription agency or Jossey-Bass directly.